QUIRKY KING'S LYNN

Bill Lovelock

AMBERLEY

This book is for my grandchildren, Elliot, Harvey and Lilly.

First published 2026

Amberley Publishing
The Hill, Stroud
Gloucestershire, GL5 4EP

www.amberley-books.com

British Library Cataloguing in Publication Data.
A catalogue record for this book is available from the British Library.

ISBN 978 1 3981 3248 1 (paperback)
ISBN 978 1 3981 3249 8 (ebook)

Origination by Amberley Publishing.
Typeset by Simon and Sons ITES Services Pvt. Ltd., Chennai, India.
Printed in Great Britain.

Appointed GPSR EU Representative:
Easy Access System Europe Oü, 16879218
Address: Mustamäe tee 50, 10621, Tallinn, Estonia
Contact Details: gpsr.requests@easproject.com, +358 40 500 3575

Contents

Introduction

Kings Lynn is Norfolk's second biggest conurbation after the city of Norwich. Many think of it as a modern London overspill town of no historical or architectural merit, but nothing could be further from the truth. Previously known as Bishop's Lynn prior to the Reformation, it has a long history as a port and a member of the early 'Common Market' trading organisation the 'Hanseatic League'. Nicholas Pevsner devotes over thirty pages to Lynn and four perambulations in his renowned 'Buildings of England' series. His opening words are 'the historic core of Kings Lynn is delightful'. These 'delightful' buildings do, however, hide tales of ghosts, ghouls and witches, as well as marks of burst hearts, devils' feet and preserved skulls. A group of experts recently estimated that one site has at least thirty-seven resident ghosts. This book will fill in the quirky background to these legends and fables.

Religion has not really been a calming influence on the town. In early medieval times it was a hotbed of religious thought with most examples of friars and monks being represented. This even included brethren who were coffin sleepers and other hermits known as anchorites who would undergo the service of the dead before they were walled in. Some of these refused to leave their cells even when pirates or looters were pillaging their towns and consequently burned to death when the church was torched. Mephistopheles arrived in Lynn by ship and went ashore to gather some souls. He was then, fortunately, spotted by a priest who cornered him, with interesting results. A learned medieval scholar from Lynn allegedly travelled alone to the North Pole and later made five further Arctic expeditions. How true this is can be discovered from reading on, as well as secret tunnels, disappearing fiddlers and an artist who painted with acid on nylon and influenced 'The Who'; a mystic, visionary and pilgrim from Lynn in the Middle Ages who had the 'gift of tears' and travelled to the Holy Land, Assisi, Rome and Santiago di Compostela whilst preventing an ancient building from destruction by fire purely by prayer; and one man's legacy for all time bequeathed in a building he paid for to be built, where that perpetuity lasted less than forty years. A fine structure connects the £5 note, the North West Passage and Al Pacino.

As you can see, this town, with its unique atmosphere, has many stories to tell. The author has walked the streets of the historic centre on many occasions and it is totally possible to lose oneself into times gone by and to imagine being an explorer, naval officer or even a religious personage from long ago. This is why the town has been used for television and movie filming on numerous occasions. By the efforts of the local council, preservation groups and eminent personages, a huge amount of history has been preserved and enhanced. Several themed guides to various aspects of the town are available from the Tourist Office and the many museums are all well worth a visit.

Eccentrics, Auto-destructive Art and a Secret Society

Eccentrics

Thomas Kent

On 15 February 1910, the *Lincolnshire Echo* reported that, in the King's Lynn Police Court before the mayor, Charles William Perry, and other magistrates, an elderly man, Thomas Kent, seventy-eight years of age, appeared before the bench. He was well known around the town as an eccentric character. On the previous Sunday he had called at the mayor's residence, Sedgeford Hall, some 15 miles from Lynn, and caused some annoyance whilst asking for a cup of tea. He had also called at the Town Hall that morning in order to see the aforementioned mayor. He was informed that he must not keep annoying people as he had been reported by several other residents. Kent asserted he had not done any such thing. Mr F. J. Miles, one of the magistrates, retorted 'then what made you call me up at a quarter to three the other morning to ask me the time?'

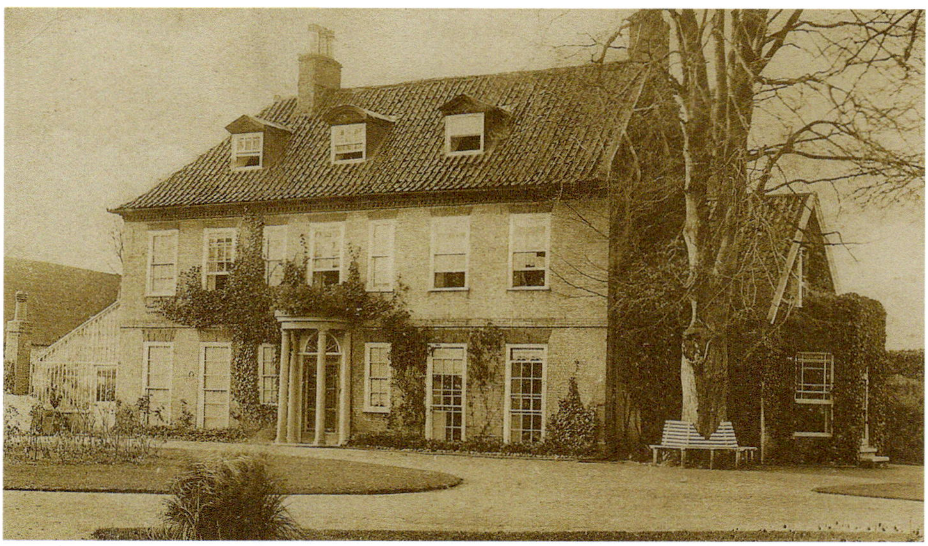

Sedgeford Hall. Scene of an unwelcome visitor. (By kind permission of the Peter Maleczek collection)

Kent was warned that if there were any further complaints made against him, he could face further action. It had been reported that on nomination day for the recent Parliamentary election, Kent had handed in to the Town Clerk a purported nomination paper on his behalf and now believed he was the Member for the Borough. Charles William Perry was a well-respected man in the town, a charity trustee, magistrate, hospital governor and proprietor of Jermyn and Perry drapers. He later moved with his family to take control of 'Longleys' of Aylesbury, drapers and outfitters. He died there in 1934 aged seventy-seven.

Penny Farthings

A sixty-eight-year-old penny farthing rider from King's Lynn was one of 140 cyclists who helped break numerous world records on Sunday 13 October 2024. A high-wheel bicycle (also known as a penny farthing, high wheeler and ordinary) is a type of bicycle with a large front wheel and a much smaller rear wheel that was popular in the 1880s. It is now generally accepted that the penny farthing had its origins in France in the 1860s, although British inventor James Starley has been described as the 'father of the cycle industry', having been involved in its continued development. The penny farthing came after the development of the 'Hobbyhorse', and the French 'Velocipede' or 'Boneshaker, all

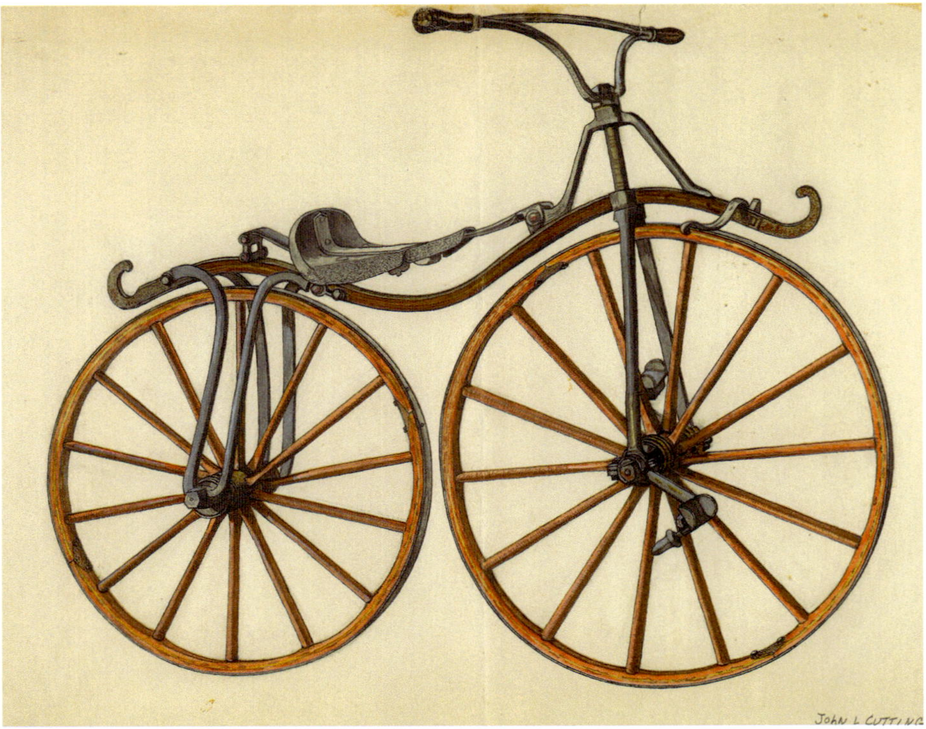

An early bicycle. The aptly named 'boneshaker'. John Cutting, 1935–42. (National Gallery of Art)

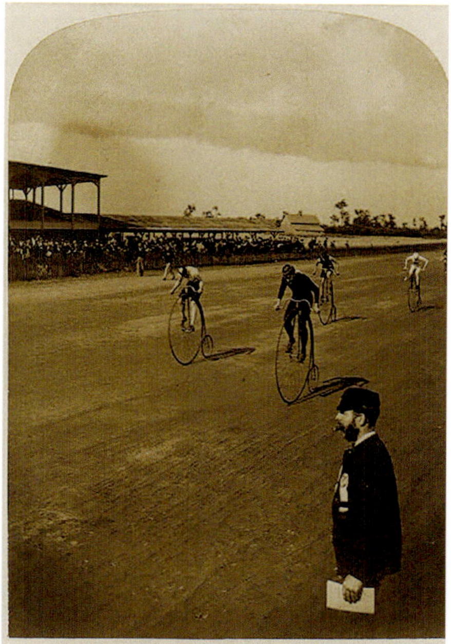

L. A. W.—Bicycle Race—Ordinary—The Finish.

'L.A.W. Bicycle Race – Ordinary–The Finish', *c.* 1890, by Geo. Barker. (Library of Congress)

versions of early bikes. However, the penny farthing was the first really efficient machine, consisting of a small rear wheel and large front wheel pivoting on a simple tubular frame with tyres of rubber. Brian Cobbold from King's Lynn started riding a penny farthing five years ago after he got back into cycling following retirement from the police. The Guinness World Record event saw broadcaster Jeremy Vine take part. Mr Cobbold said it was not something to be missed. The event, which attracted people from the United States and across Europe, was held at Herne Hill Velodrome before riders cycled to the Queen Elizabeth Olympic Park Velodrome. Twelve world records by the group and individuals were broken during the event, including for the largest number of penny farthing racers in a velodrome. Mr Cobbold said riding the Victorian-era cycle was a great way of keeping fit, physically and mentally. He was among other riders dressed in tweed and top hats at the event, which he described as 'eccentric'. There were about fifty-five riders on the 12-mile trip through central London.

Juggling Jim

A man pronounced dead in a property in Nelson Street on 23 January 2017 was a much-loved street entertainer. A post-mortem revealed he had died of pneumonia aged sixty-two. Known to generations of Lynn residents as 'Juggling Jim', he was a familiar sight strumming his battered guitar, with broken strings, or performing juggling tricks which always seemed to go wrong. His usual pitch was near Next in Lynn's High Street, although he took a break from Lynn sometimes to perform outside the Spar shop in Hunstanton High Street. His real name was Anthony Bowen. He was born in Magdalen, King's Lynn, in 1955 and had been involved with the King's Lynn Players in the 1980s. A tribute pinned to the door where he performed said: 'Juggling Jim rest in peace. The show is over, you got a standing ovation. You will be missed'. Bunches of flowers, juggling clubs and hoops were left by well wishers. In 2016, he told a YouTube documentary filmed by College of West Anglia student Brodie Rake: 'I get called all sorts of things up here. Juggling Jim's the one most people know me as, or "Old Jim" sometimes.'

He revealed he had been married but his wife passed away. He said his second partner who he lived with had a terminal illness but walked out on him. He told Mister Rake that he lived off his performances. 'It makes me a living, it's not too bad,' he said. 'It's a routine, it's a structured performance.'

In the documentary, named *The Enigma of Juggling Jim,* he said he liked to write songs and plays in his spare time and go the cinema. His favourite movie was *Back to the Future II.* When asked what the key to happiness was, he said: 'Just do your own thing, do what you want to do.'

The town paid its last respects at a packed minster, on the Saturday Market Place, and the service was arranged for free by Lynn-based funeral directors A. J. Coggles to give Mr Bowen a dignified send-off. He was buried at Gayton church, alongside his father Leonard, who died just over a fortnight before him, on Saturday 5 February 2017. West Norfolk Council has said a plaque could be put up to remember Mr Bowen in the doorway where he performed but to date

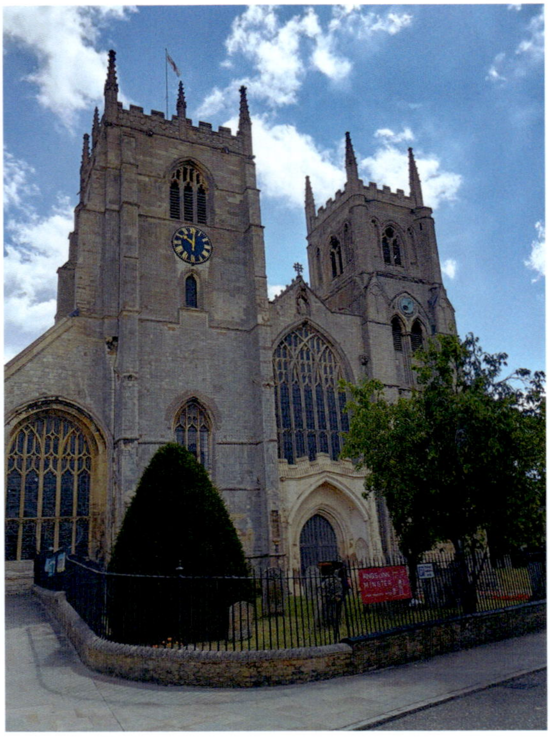

St Margaret's Church, King's Lynn, the King's Lynn Minster since 2011.

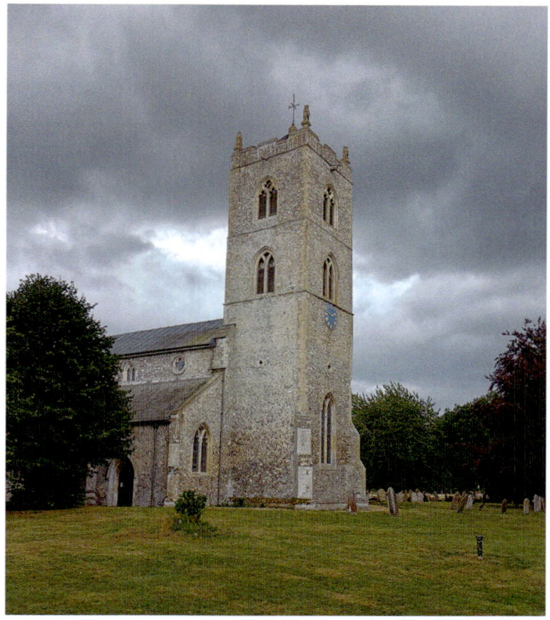

Gayton church, a thirteenth-century Grade I listed building popular for weddings.

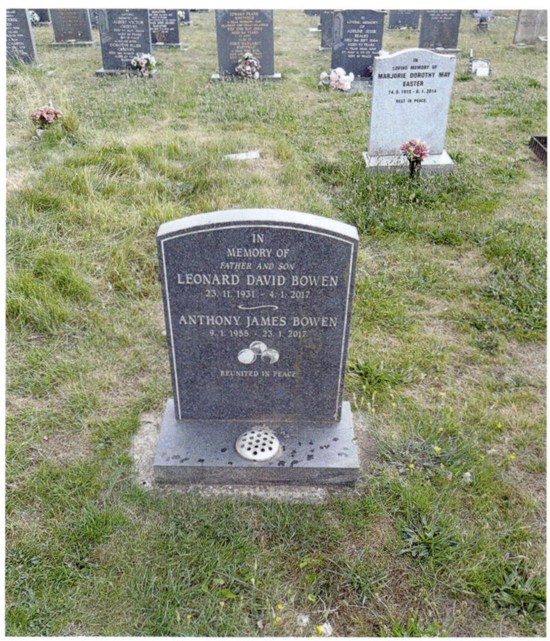

Father and son reunited at Gayton church.

this has not been done. However, in collaboration with The Norfolk Brewhouse, limited edition bottles in memory of 'Juggling Jim' were available to purchase, with all the profits going to charity. Versions of Moon Gazer Ruby, Gold and Amber had special commemorative labels on to celebrate Anthony and the impact he had on the town.

The Fifth Duke of Portland

Originally known as Lord John Bentinck, the Fifth Duke (1800–79) followed in the family tradition when he entered the world of politics as the Conservative MP for King's Lynn between 1824 and 1826. The Bentinck dock, in King's Lynn, was opened in 1883 by the Sixth Duke and named in recognition of the family that had often represented the town in Parliament. There is a Bentinck Arms pub in North Lynn, which also opened in 1883. Despite being a firm supporter of the Tory party, the Fifth Duke was never especially politically active, and spoke infrequently in both Houses of Parliament. He was educated at home. Despite suffering from delicate health, he served in the army from 1818, reaching the rank of captain in the Grenadier Guards by 1830. As a younger son, he was not originally destined to succeed to the title, but on the death of his brother, William Henry, in 1824, he became Marquess of Titchfield and heir to his father's dukedom. He allowed over three years to elapse after his accession to the dukedom before he took his seat in the House of Lords, not taking the oaths until 5 June 1857. He had been offered the Order of the Garter, but declined it, and refused it again in 1877.

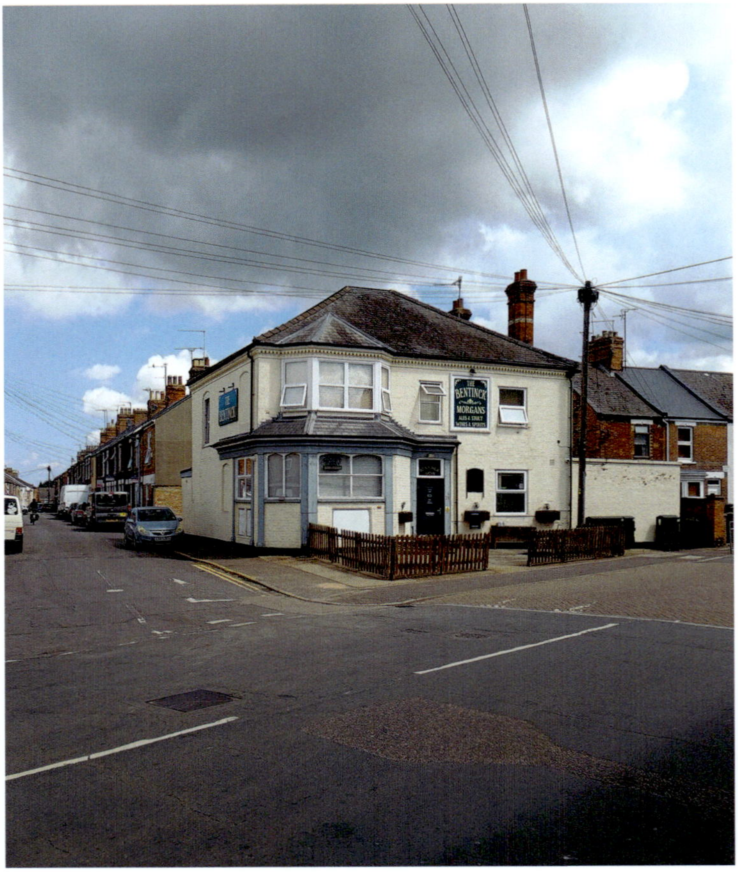

Bentinck Arms, King's Lynn, one of the legacies of the Dukes of Portland.

He was extremely fond of the opera and courted the singer Adelaide Kemble. In fact, he proposed to Adelaide, but was turned down by her. He had enjoyed something of a public life up until this setback, but having been rejected by the chanteuse, his unconventional behaviour apparently increased. Eventually his eccentricities became famous. Most notably, he was so severely introverted that he refused contact with any person other than his valet and insisted on conducting all his affairs by post. He would also carry an umbrella at all times, rain or shine, to hide behind, should anyone acknowledge him on his excursions into the outside world. He was known as the 'burrowing duke' and was responsible for commissioning an extraordinary range of buildings and a system of tunnels below the Welbeck estate, particularly an underground network of galleries, rooms and passages that were only ever used by the duke himself. Although his motives for carrying out these works were undoubtedly eccentric, he was also known to be a good employer by the standards of his time, and may have been deliberately using his fortune to create work and offer secure incomes to local people. He was also the man behind the creation of the estate's kitchen gardens, the biggest in Britain. He provided his employees with umbrellas and donkeys to enable them to get to and from work without fatigue, and when roller skating first became popular, he had a rink installed near the lake for the benefit of the staff and he encouraged them to make good use of it. Similarly, he liked them to row on the lake and would sometimes coach them in oarsmanship.

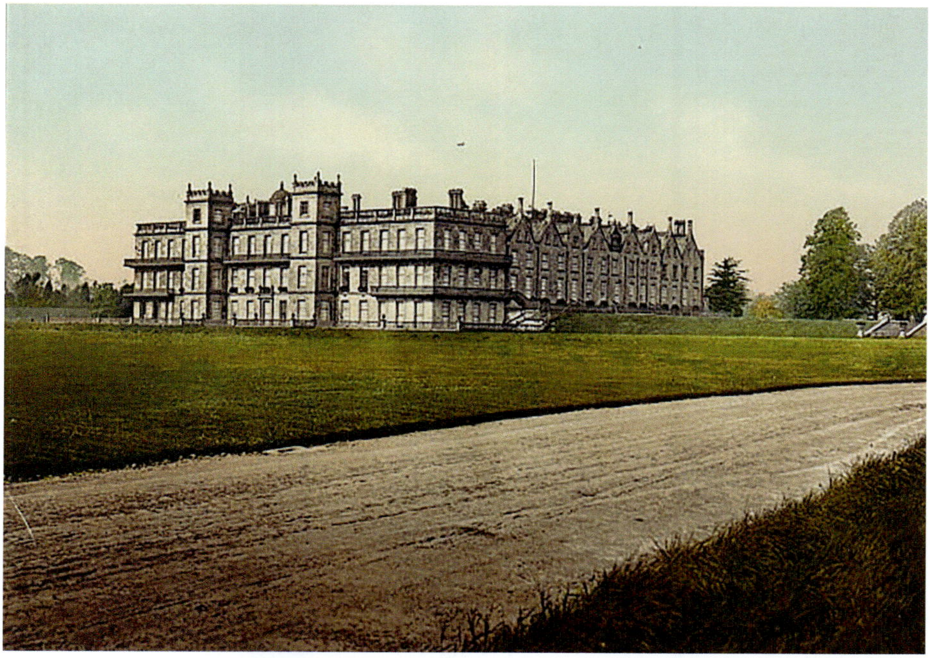

Welbeck estate around 1890 to 1906. Even bigger, probably, under the ground. (Library of Congress)

Among his building projects was a vast riding house lit by 4,000 gas lamps, to serve the one hundred horses kept in his stables. He never used it. An underground ballroom was excavated and furnished beneath Welbeck Abbey, its ceiling painted with a huge sunset, but no one was ever invited to a ball or danced there during his lifetime. A tunnel led to Worksop and was broad enough for two carriages. He was sometimes rumoured to keep a pet mole that he would stroke for comfort when under stress. Mick Jackson's *The Underground Man,* a novel shortlisted for the Booker Prize in 1997, features a fictionalised version of the duke as its main character. The interiors on the Welbeck estate during his time were almost all painted pink. Pink was, at this time, believed to be the more masculine colour, the softer tone of blue more appropriate for girls. These associations were only changed in the 1920s. The Fifth Duke never married. He was succeeded by his cousin, William Cavendish-Bentinck, a grandson of the Third Duke, in 1896.

After the duke's death, an application was made by the widow of Walter Thomas Druce, son of the late Thomas Charles Druce, the owner of Baker Street Bazaar, London, for T. C. Druce's body to be exhumed from the Druce family vault at Highgate Cemetery. She claimed that her father-in-law, T. C. Druce, was in fact the Fifth Duke of Portland, who had worked as an upholsterer for some years then staged a sham burial as Druce in 1864. The coffin would, therefore, be empty. One of the difficulties in disproving the claim was the lack of visual records of the Duke of Portland, the recluse who had shunned public contact. A photograph of a bust was finally submitted as evidence of his appearance. The case to claim the Portland inheritance was continued by members of the Druce family for some years after Mrs Druce was admitted to a mental home in 1903. A company was set up to support the case with a capital of over £30,000 subscribed by the public in expectation of huge profits. The coffin was finally opened in 1907 and was found indeed to contain the body of T. C. Druce. The Druce-Portland Company, and the legal case, collapsed. An episode in the 1976 television series *Victorian Scandals* featured the events as 'The Portland Millions' with Nigel Havers.

The Wandering Piper

On Monday 12 November 1832, the 'Wandering Piper' arrived in Lynn and with permission of the mayor, played in the streets for two days. He performed at the 'Freemason's Tavern' on the Monday evening and at the 'Crown Tavern' on the Tuesday evening, both now demolished. Apparently playing as the result of a wager, he donated £2 15*s* 8*d* to the Lynn Dispensary and vouchers had been seen showing upwards of £700 had been given to charitable institutions and destitute individuals. 'There were many contradictory remarks about the eccentric behaviour of the gentleman, the wise may smile, the benevolent must rejoice at the laborious task undertaken, a few months will, in all probability,

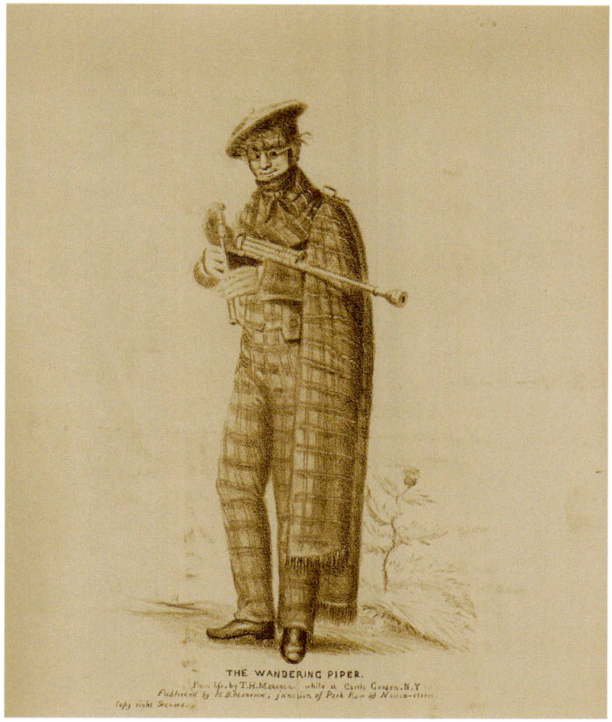

The 'Wandering Piper', a lithograph of a drawing by Thomas Charles Wageman *c.* 1833. Although contemporary, it has never been confirmed that this is the man himself. (Library of Congress)

clear up whatever mystery at present hangs over this benevolent individual'. In the spring of 1829, the mystery of the 'Wandering Piper' had begun. Regional newspapers had been established in many towns and cities across Britain and fortunately many accounts of his travels were recorded. He travelled the length and breadth of the land from Brighton to Berwick, and Scotland and Ireland collecting for charity and his keep. Very large sums were raised in this way. In 1834 he was in Montreal, Canada, and even visited New York, New York. In Lincolnshire in December 1829 an old woman gave him a penny, saying 'I know you, my lord'. Although this was denied by the piper, it only added to the mystery. In 1833 the piper, described as a tall, gaunt figure between fifty and sixty years of age, suffered injuries from an overturned stagecoach and recuperated for fifteen months at the mansion of Sir Thomas Butler in Carlow, Ireland. His travels continued and, finally, in 1837, he wrote a letter to the 'British Public' in which his story was revealed. In 1824 at the London Coffee House, a wager had been struck. The piper would travel with his border pipes throughout Britain and the United States collecting for charities and his friend would do the same through France playing a fiddle. The winner would be he who collected the most monies. The piper announced his name as Graham Stuart. Sadly, in February 1839, Mr. Stuart passed away after a three week stay in the Mercers Hospital in Dublin. He left all his property to that institution.

Auto-destructive Art

Gustav Metzger

Gustav Metzger (1926–2017) was an activist, campaigner, anti-capitalist, junk dealer and artist. It is little known that this internationally renowned artist lived and worked in King's Lynn between 1950 and 1959. His exhibition there, 'Treasures of East Anglian Churches' in 1957, was exhibited in the fourteenth-century crypt of Clifton House. Damaged relics told the story of iconoclasm as a result of the English Reformation. That exhibition marked the beginning of his interest in the relationship between destruction and creation, and he made his first auto-destructive artwork, painting with acid onto nylon, in the town. Sixty-two years later, a second exhibition, 'Destroy, and you Create' showed paintings and drawings from Metzger's years in Lynn where he said his activism was formed. There are two plaques dedicated to the artist situated around the town. The first, green, very informative one, is erected in St Nicholas Street, where he lived in a property at the rear, and the second, less informative, blue one at the site of his former shop and residence at No. 30 Queens Street. He arrived in England with his brother in 1939, one of nearly 10,000 refugee children rescued by the Kindertransport. He was taught from 1945 for the next eight years by David Bomberg in London at the Borough Polytechnic, now part of the London South Bank University. Initially inspired by Bomberg's political ideals and approach to art making, Metzger and his teacher severed ties in 1953, in what would become a defining event that influenced the course of his life. After spending time as an active member and chairman of the 'Borough Bottega', an artist collective formed in association with Bomberg and his other students, he fell in with the Avant Garde. Metzger created the term 'Auto-destructive Art' a movement followed by the likes

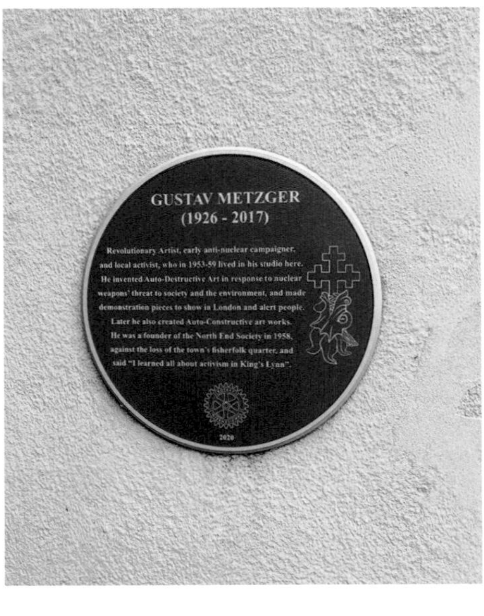

Plaque in St Nicholas Street. Gustav Metzger lived in a property at the rear of this building.

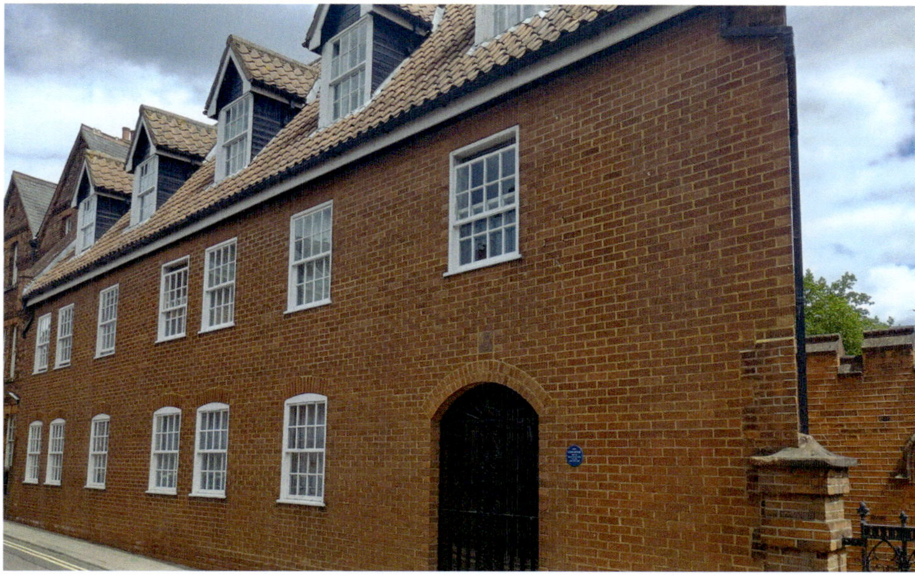

No. 30 Queens Street, a new build on the site of Gustav Metzger's residence and shop.

of guitar-trashing Pete Townshend and Yoko Ono. Guitarist Townshend of The Who studied with Metzger, and during the 1960s, Metzger's work was projected on screens at The Who concerts. Metzger also worked with Cream, providing them with light shows in the 1960s. This was campaigning art, decrying war and humanity's destructive impact on the natural environment. He was also challenging commercialism and egocentrism in art, but politics was the heart of his motivation. Metzger wanted to provide people with another vision, to see connections, to see the differences and interact. He hoped his work would stimulate and enhance daily life, which he felt happened far too fast. He is remembered more in King's Lynn for his rackety junk stall in the Corn Exchange on the Tuesday Market Place, and for campaigning to save the north end of the town, the home of the Lynn fisherfolk then under threat of demolition and gentrification. His shyness hid a determination. Politics had been his lifeblood in his teens and he became involved with the Direct Action Committee against nuclear war, including a stint in prison following his involvement with civil disobedience protests with the Committee of 100, which he co-founded with the philosopher and pacifist Bertrand Russell. His fears about men and machines were linked to his experience of Nazism, he told an interviewer in 2012, and its destruction of his family. The Gustav Metzger Foundation is a charity which was founded upon Metzger's death at the age of ninety in 2017. During his lifetime, Metzger defined the organisation's mission by envisioning not only exhibitions of his work and furtherance of the political and philosophical ideas he espoused, but also through support for individuals working in the fields of the arts and environmental studies, and for initiatives 'to combat the risk of global extinction arising from the activities of humans.'

A Secret Society

The Sons of Reffley

King's Lynn was the site of an unusual secret society based around a mineral spring. Mineral springs have long been sites of worship, holding particular importance for the Romans who built temples and shrines dedicated to them. It was believed they had healing powers and that drinking the water could revitalise the mind and body. In part this was true, due to the cleanliness and high mineral content of the water. In the eighteenth century, chalybeate springs became the latest health fad due to their iron content, which was thought to have therapeutic properties. In the Gaywood River valley, several of these springs were known to exist and a secret society, known as the Sons of Reffley, emerged. They venerated the mineral springs in the area, serving members a punch containing its healing waters. Before being cleared for housing, the woods formed one single expanse of trees. Local historians believe the Reffley brethren may have eventually left the woods in the nineteenth century and instead became a drinking club, frequenting the many taverns in King's Lynn. The temple was later demolished, but the secret society

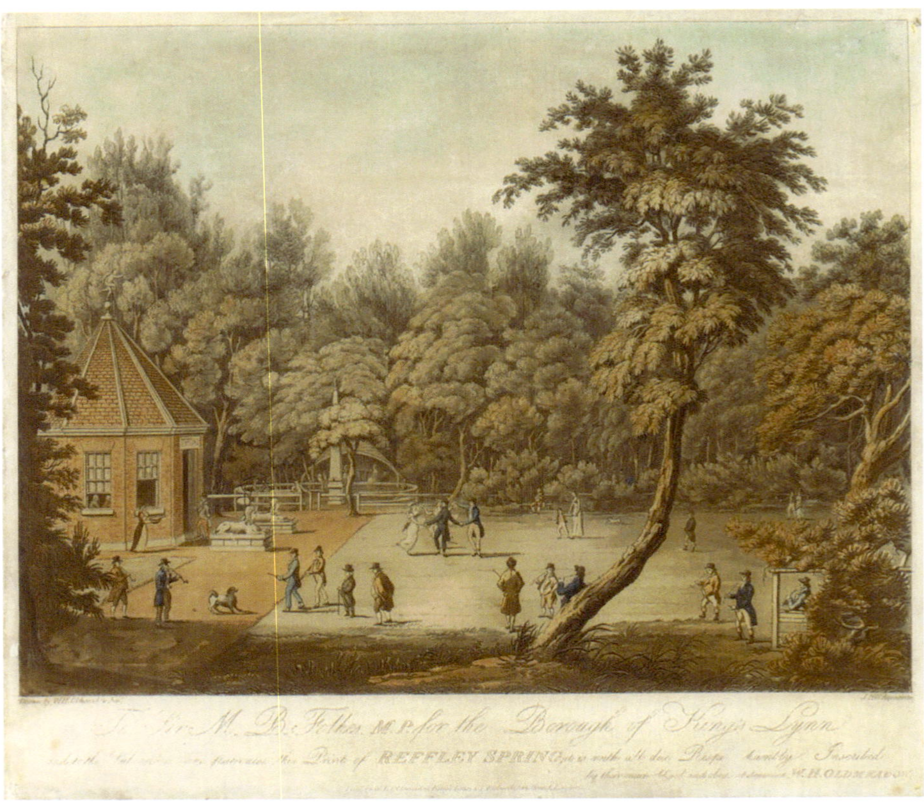

Oil painting showing Reffley Spring by J. Hill, active nineteenth century after W. H. Oldmeadow (1841–49). (Yale Center for British Art)

is understood to still meet to this day. Their number was strictly limited to thirty, supposedly based on the Cromwellian edict which banned the assembly of more than thirty men. It is believed the group was descended from an earlier society formed in 1650, the year after the execution of King Charles I, and that over the years the group's role moved from political to social. The men would drink a secret punch made from the spring water, meet, eat a beef joint, saddle of mutton and a lobster salad and then smoke a secret blend of tobacco in the clay pipes that members were all presented with. An oil painting from 1800 shows an octagonal temple with a conical roof, although this building was enlarged in 1832 when a kitchen was added to the back. Two sphinxes guarded the temple and along with the obelisk, brought a flavour of the Valley of the Kings to this secluded spot in the west of the county. By the first half of the nineteenth century, the spring had started to lose its place in high society as the railways came and carried people away from the west. But the Reffley Brethren still came. In an article in the *Eastern Daily Press* of 22 September 1936, an article was written about the brethren and their temple:

> Many are the folk who have questioned the secrets of the Latin-inscribed obelisk and the mysterious, locked and shuttered little building which unexpectedly comes to view ... Once a year, at least, there enters its doors a group of jovial men, the privileged brethren of this society. Each July, and sometimes again in autumn, they come to this spot to breathe the old-world atmosphere of their temple feast and drink their punch of unknown recipe.

In 1936, the head was the Reverend Sir Frances ffolkes, who ensured that the temple was never entered by any of the sons unless they had drunk from the spring and then downed two glasses of spring water punch. The punch was, at that time, made to a recipe known only to the honorary brewer, a position held by a Mr D'Oyly-Watkins and the secretary, Mr Cawson, also known as 'Father Reffley', a position which involved ensuring the society's customs were observed. Cawson took over the position of secretary from a Mr Robinson Cruso, a King's Lynn auctioneer who provided, it was claimed, the inspiration for Daniel Defoe's famous story of shipwrecks and adventure. An inscription on a column which rose 20 feet above the Reffley spring in front of the temple noted that it replaced an older column and that the spring beneath it had been consecrated on 24 June 1756. In Latin, on one side of the obelisk read: 'We dedicate this sacred fountain of happiness, these waters of joy to Bacchus and Venus, and the gods of this place.' On another: 'Whoever upholds this column or gives order that it be upheld may he live longer than anyone else in his generation' and also 'if you wish to relinquish your load of care, go to whatever place is full of pleasure. Let this be your labour. Let this be your care. Let us all go, both little and big, if we wish that Venus and Bacchus shall love us.' The secret brew was taken from ancient china pots, from willow-patterned punch bowls and a series of toasts were read. Although membership was strictly limited, the odd exception was made for visitors. King George V lunched at the temple before his accession. Women were only allowed 'in the form of servants or sphinxes'. Sadly, by the late 1970s, the temple had fallen victim to vandalism. On 23 June1978, a few days after Midsummer's Night Eve, the last traditional public celebration was held at Reffley spring. The inscription on the obelisk had been translated to mean something very different by 1978. 'Whosoever shall remove this or bid its removal, let him die the last of his race.' Frightened at the thought of a curse, the Reffley estate residents' association agreed a peppercorn rent of ten pence a year to the brethren to lease the site as guardians and on the 200th anniversary of the gift of the society's stone picnic table, they met. There was feasting, music-making, magic acts and fancy-dress competitions: they ate rabbit and gravy pie, red cabbage salads, Norfolk hot potatoes, gooseberry tansy and 'very good wigs, the most delightful things for tea'. Wigs, or Wiggs, are loaves or cakes made with yeast, butter and eggs and flavoured with caraway seeds and were normally eaten with ale and cheese. They are still very popular in Yorkshire. Despite the brethren's best efforts, within a decade, the temple had been pulled down, the obelisk demolished and the sphinxes removed to a secret location. The spring dried out and all that remains today is the remains of a spa basin. Today, the site of the temple and the basin is in private woodland and is overgrown – perhaps the spring remains dry, perhaps it will one day flow again.

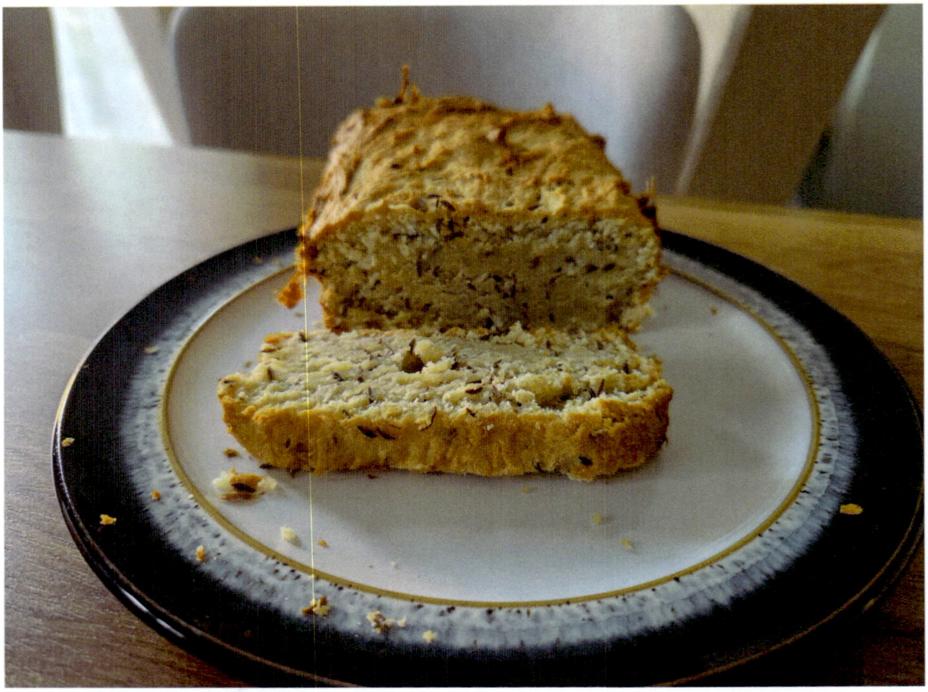

Wiggs Loaf, baked and photographed by Mark and Sarah Mantle. (Courtesy of Harvey Mantle)

Anchorites, Coffin Sleepers, Exorcists and a Stalker

Anchorites

The present-day All Saints' Church in King's Lynn was re-established on the site of a Saxon structure in 1095 and is the town's oldest building. It has an anchorage cell, a space for a solitary religious hermit. This cell, located on the south wall of the chancel, housed both male and female anchorites and anchoresses, who dedicated their lives to prayer and devotion. The cell offers a glimpse into the lives of these individuals who lived in seclusion within the church walls. The current cell dates from around 1500, and anchorites were present at the church from the thirteenth to fifteenth centuries. There was also one at the Blackfriars Priory Church in the town. Anchorites, sometimes referred to as 'desert dwellers', were religious recluses who chose to live a solitary life, often in a dedicated cell or enclosure, for spiritual reasons. Some refused to leave their cells even when pirates or looters were pillaging their towns and consequently burned to death when the church was torched. The practice originated with the

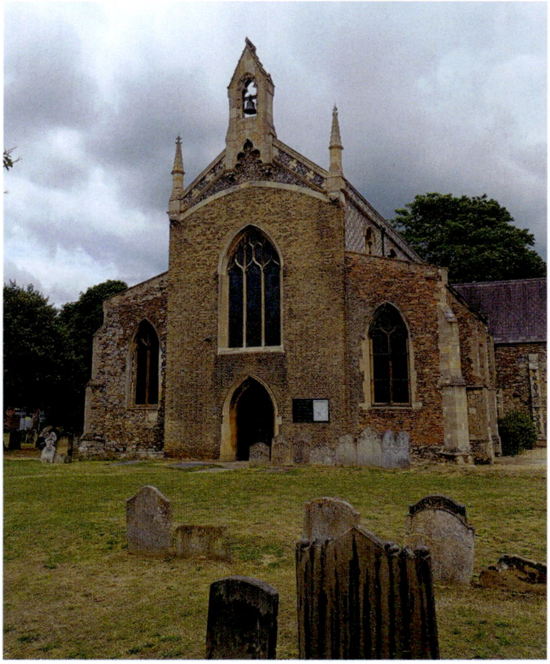

All Saints' Church, the site of the anchorite cell.

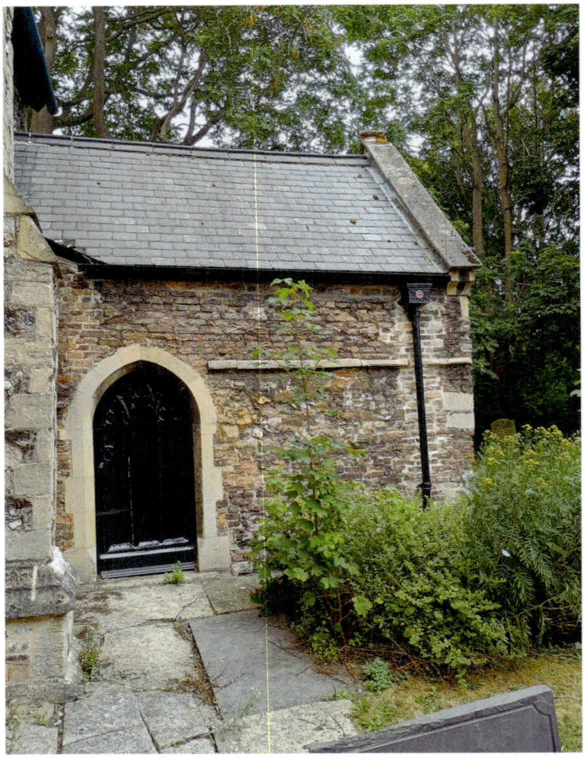

Left: The exterior of the anchorite cell at All Saints' Church today.

Below: The Anchorite, 1869, by Mariano Fortuny Marsal (1838–74). (National Gallery of Art)

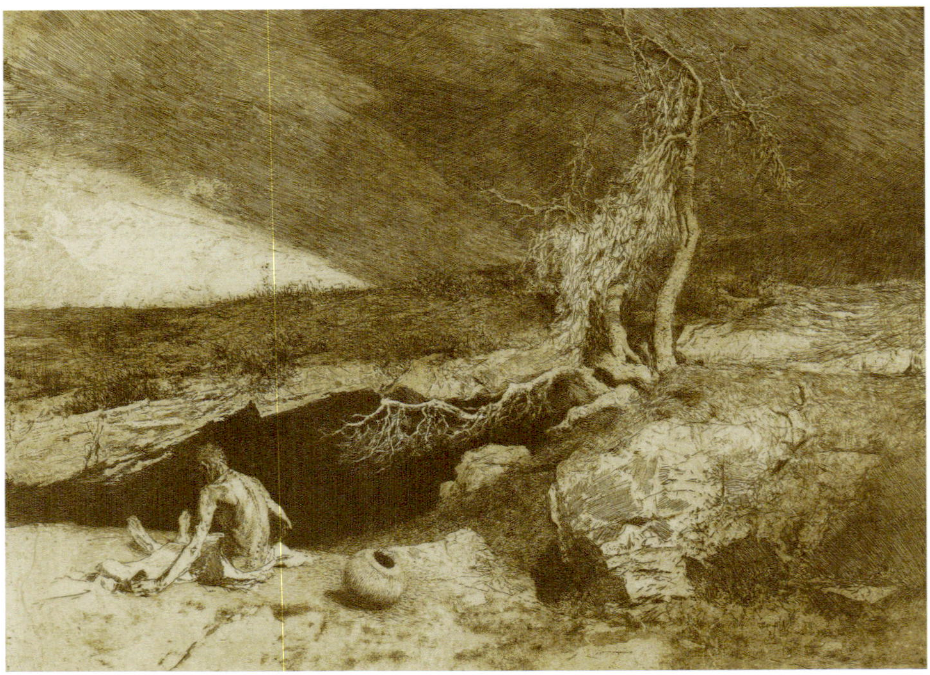

early Christians who withdrew to the desert and it evolved into a widespread tradition in Europe during the Middle Ages. There have likely been anchorites and anchoresses in England since the first conversions, but none were recorded before the eleventh century. From then on, it was an idea that flourished rapidly for a few centuries, but largely dying out with the Reformation and the country shifting from Catholicism to the more pragmatic Protestantism. It was quite an enclosed life, lived for years in a single stone room which was usually built on to the side of a church, with a single shuttered slit through to the body of the church so the anchorite could receive communion and take part in services. Those who chose to be anchorites quite literally left life as we live it – the service of the dead was given before they were walled in. They used chamber pots which were passed through an opening to a servant, who would also bring food. These servants were paid – being a recluse was not something for the poor. But in those days, most, but certainly not all, of those who went into convents and monasteries came from well-to-do families who made gifts to the institutions. In England, Julian of Norwich is probably the best known of the anchorites. Her book, *Revelations of Divine Love*, is the earliest extant example of a book written by a woman in the English language, and even today it remains widely read. Her phrase 'All shall be well, and all shall be well and all manner of thing shall be well' has become a part of the general lexicon.

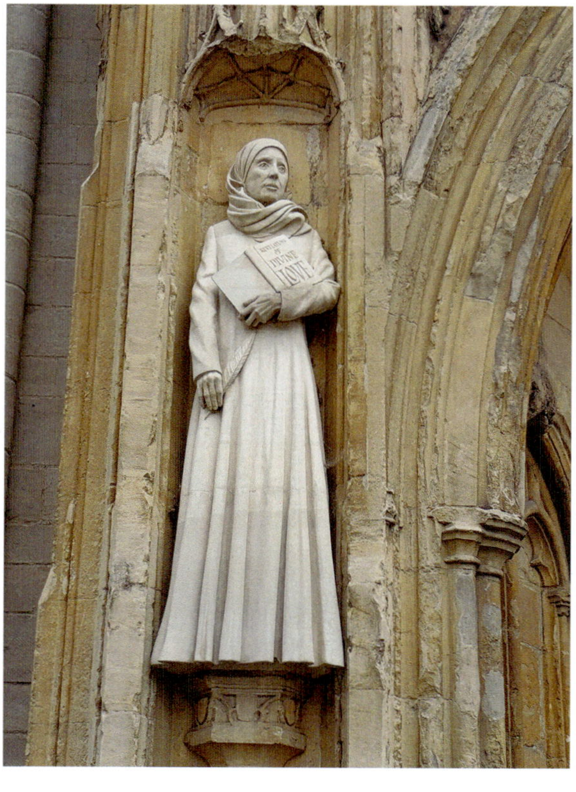

Julian of Norwich. This statue was created in 2001 by sculptor David Holgate and stands outside the west door of Norwich Cathedral.

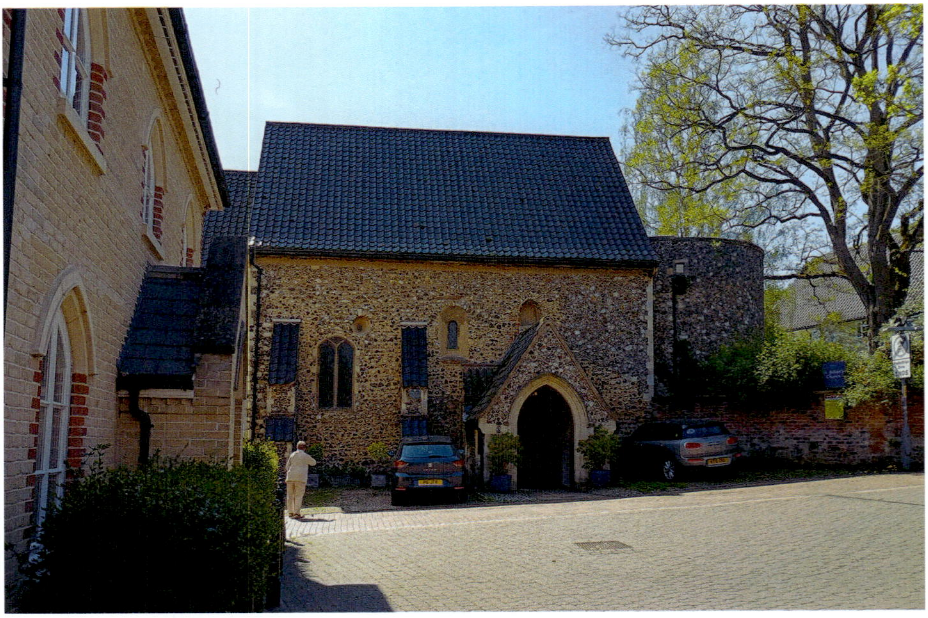

The beautiful Norwich church that was the site of St Julian's cell.

Coffin Sleepers

The Friars of the Penitence of Jesus Christ, popularly known as the Sack Friars, were a mendicant movement formed in Provence in the 1240s, inspired by the teaching of Franciscans. Their unofficial name must refer to the sack-like cloth they wore, and reveals the emphasis the friars placed on humility and poverty. They had their feet bare and wore wooden sandals. Their mode of life was very austere, and they never ate meat and drank only water. The practice of sleeping in coffins was a stark symbol of their commitment to living in the present and reflecting on mortality. The coffins were not just a place to sleep, but a constant reminder of their own eventual death, promoting a sense of reflection and humility. The order was known for its eccentric habits and beliefs, with the coffin sleeping practice being a prominent example. The Sack Friars apparently planned their move into England in 1256 and they arrived the following year. They set up their first English house in London. There is a plaque in Norwich which suggests an earlier date. The Friars of the Sack, or '*De Penitentia*', had a house in King's Lynn in the thirteenth century. The exact site is not definitely known but it was probably in the vicinity of 'Greenland Fisheries' in Bridge Street. The order, which never attained too much prosperity, was suppressed in France in 1293, the members being obliged to join the Austin Friars in consequence of the smallness of their numbers. In England they came to an end in 1317, when the members were obliged to join one or other of the four chief orders of the mendicants. Despite the popular support and their great number, these friars were simply too holy and humble to consider contesting a decree of the Church.

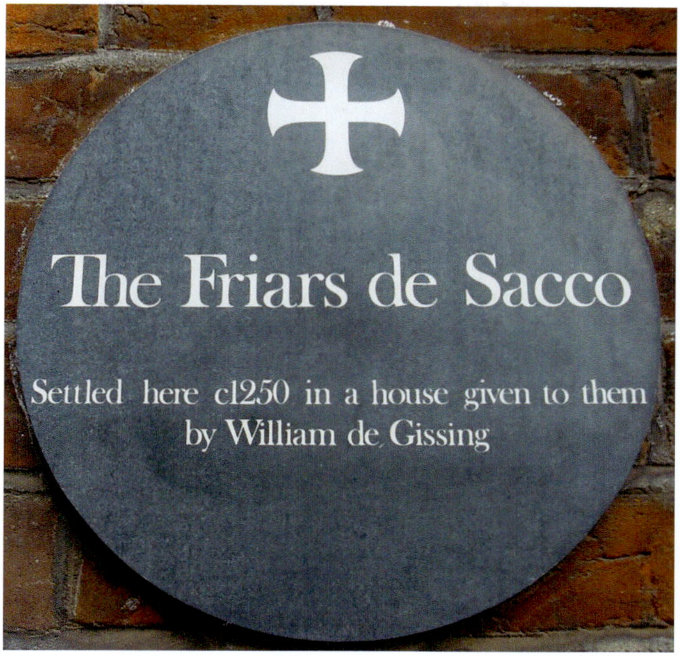

Plaque in Elm Hill, Norwich, marking the Sack Friars.

In 1993 it was reported that in Sihastria, a monastery in Romania, there were no beds for the monks. Everyone slept on floor on old mats or on chairs, and some of them were sleeping in coffins. The monastery was founded by Daniil Sihastrul in 1514. It has been apparently 450 years since anyone ate meat there. A parallel with the disbanded Sack Friars. In Poland there is a coffin-shaped church which was part of a monastery built in 1380 by a group of Carthusian monks from Bohemia. The small brotherhood was rather eccentric and also had a macabre custom of sleeping in coffins. The inside of the building has a sombre atmosphere. The clock is particularly dark; an angel clutching the Grim Reaper's scythe hangs from its pendulum, which is inscribed with the foreboding message 'each passing second brings you closer to your death'. Rows of carved wooden seats cover the floor and religious artwork lines the walls. The church is the largest surviving old Carthusian monastery, and is also the best-preserved Carthusian church in Poland.

Since 2005, Wat Prommanee, a Buddhist monastery in Thailand, has offered its unique services selling troubled worshippers the chance to leave their problems behind by climbing into a coffin, 'dying' and re-emerging as a new person. Every week thousands of customers flock to the monastery in Nakhon Nayok to get a fresh start in life. They pay around £3 each for floral offerings and a cash donation to the monks. Inside the monastery hall nine pink coffins with gaudy gold mouldings are lined up. 'It's five minutes sleep in the box,' explained a teacher at the monastery school. 'People want to be happy' Analysts say that in uncertain times there are growing numbers of people with problems they would rather leave behind. 'Dying', they believe, allows them to get rid of their bad karma and move on. Certainly, if you can leave a coffin on your own two feet, things are already looking up.

Exorcists

The Exorcist's House, 8 Chapel Lane, is in the grounds of St Nicholas' Chapel and is Grade II listed. The building dates from 1635 and is thought to replace an earlier building which was home to members of the clergy who served St Nicholas' Chapel. Exorcism can be defined as 'the attempt to cast an unwanted spiritual entity out of the body of a human being'. It is found in many different religions and cultures, for example, in a number of passages in the Bible, Jesus is shown casting out demons and evil spirits that have possessed unfortunate people. Many Christian saints have been associated with exorcism, such as Saint Francis of Assisi, who is sometimes depicted driving demons out of possessed people. People suffering from what we might today describe as a mental illness or a disability were sometimes considered to be possessed. The popular image of the exorcist, a priest specially trained to drive out demons, as portrayed in the character of Lankester Merrin played by the fine actor Max von Sydow in the 1973 film *The Exorcist,* bears little resemblance to the practice of exorcism in the medieval

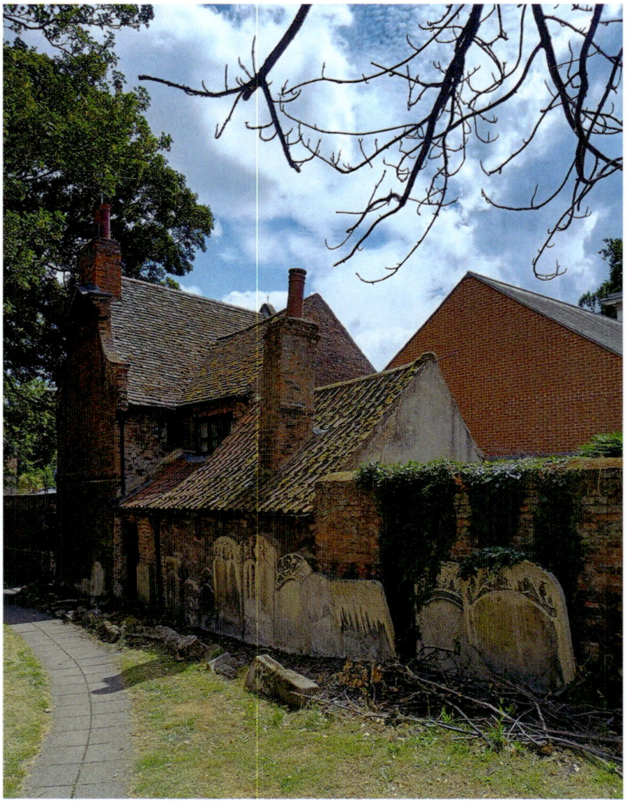

The Exorcist's House.

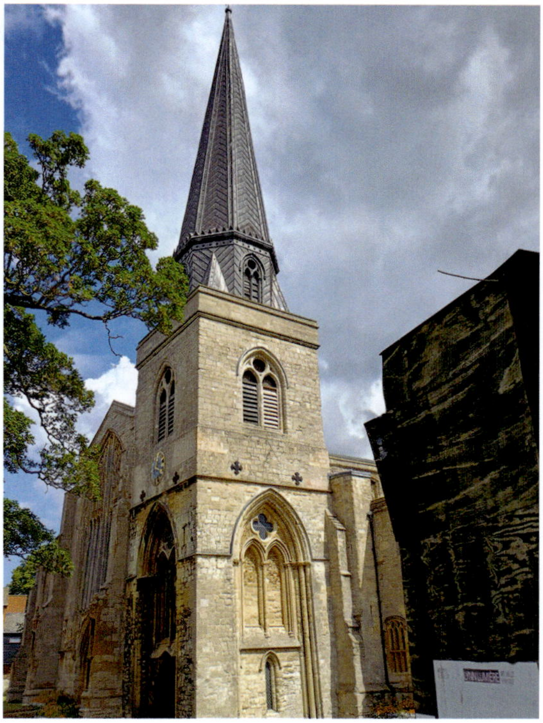

St Nicholas' Chapel next door to the Exorcist's House.

period, when those believed to be possessed by demons were encouraged to pray to saints associated with exorcism, or visit their tombs or relics. It might be that someone who once lived at the Exorcist's House, or in a previous building on the site, had been known locally as someone who had cleansed a person or a place of a malign spirit. It could have been a local clergyman whose prayers or other activities brought comfort and peace to people who felt they were troubled by evil spirits or demons. The position of exorcist was one a Catholic priest could hold as he progressed in his church career. Sadly, any tales of the exorcist that the house is named after have been lost to time. The last exorcism was carried out in the town in the late Middle Ages and is said to have led to the tragic death of a woman accused of witchcraft, who was burnt in Tuesday Market Place. Legend has it that an underground passage, allegedly used by Witchfinder General Matthew Hopkins, runs from the cottage to St Ann's House, in Lynn. Matthew Hopkins (d. 1647) was an English witch hunter and more information about him and King's Lynn can be found in chapter three of this book. A curious figure took up residence in the Exorcist's House in the twentieth century. Frederick Robert Buckley, also known as F. R. Buckley, was a pulp fiction author, film scriptwriter, occasional actor and radio broadcaster. He lived for many years in the United States, and published a number of novels and short stories during the interwar years, although after his wife's death in 1931, he appears to have returned to England. After the Second World War, he was a writer and broadcaster for the

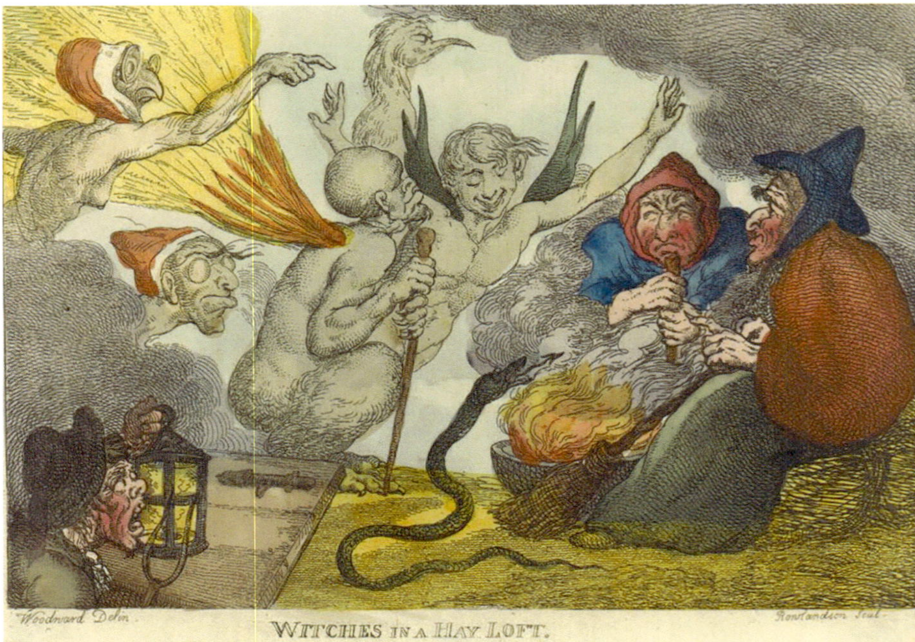

Witches in A Hayloft, *c.* 1813, by Thomas Rowlandson (1756–1827) after George Moutard Woodward (1760–1809). (Yale Center for British Art)

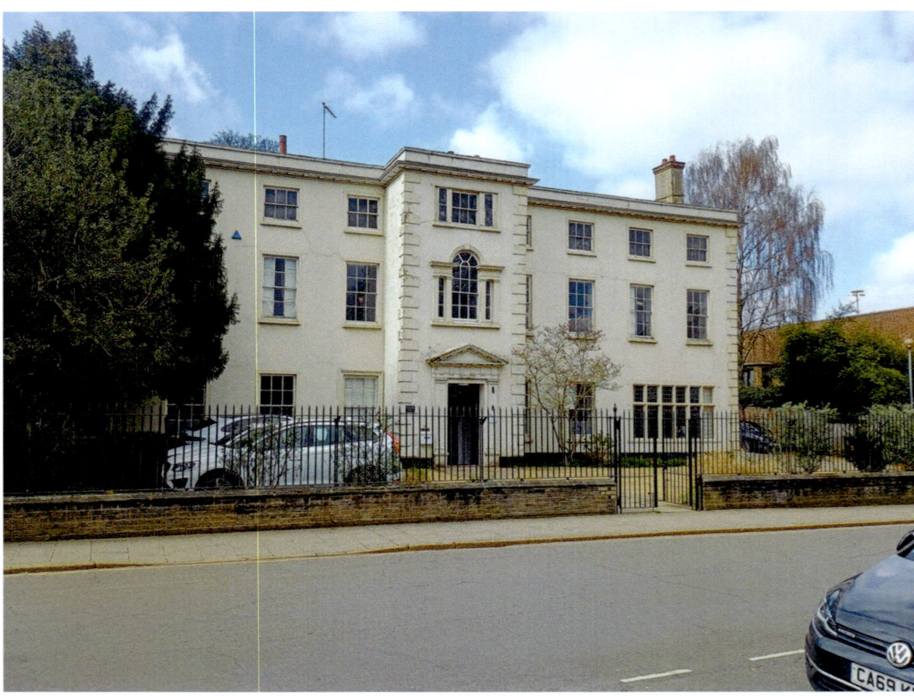

St Ann's House, head of a secret tunnel in a Grade II listed building?

BBC. In his later years, he moved to the Exorcist's House in Lynn. Little is known about Buckley, and his association with the Exorcist's House may have fuelled rumours about his interests. A young man who attempted to take a photograph of the house found that his camera shutter had jammed, and Buckley told him that he was a wizard and an expert on the occult who advised the local police about black magic rites. Buckley died in 1976, and the next residents of the Exorcist's House claimed to have seen a ghost in the cottage living room. Allegedly this was the spectre of Buckley's second wife, who had returned to America after Buckley's death, and who died on the same day that the new owner's stepdaughters reported seeing the manifestation in the Exorcist's House. The house was put up for sale in 2016, attracting attention from local and national media outlets. It is not the only house in Lynn with a long and strange history, but it continues to intrigue locals and visitors alike, featuring on local ghost walks and fuelling speculation about hauntings and dark practices. It is even referred to as the Exorcist's House in its Grade II listing by Historic England, ensuring that its mystique will continue for years to come.

A Stalker

In September 1796 a thirty-nine-year-old sea captain from King's Lynn, Captain George Vancouver, was going about his business when he was attacked with a cane near Oxford Circus on Conduit Street in Central London. He had retired on half pay to Petersham in 1795.What made the incident even more bizarre was that the Lynn man's attacker was Thomas Pitt (Lord Camelford), a member of the British aristocracy who had been stalking the victim for some time. Vancouver's civilian brother Charles intervened and gave Pitt blow after blow until onlookers restrained the attacker. Charges and counter charges flew in the press, with the wealthy Camelford faction having the greater firepower until Vancouver, ailing from his long naval service, died. The victim had recently returned from a successful exploration of the Pacific region. Vancouver's expedition was the first to produce detailed charts of the waters around the City of Vancouver and the city was named after him. He has several other places and mountains named after him, including Vancouver Island, as well as Vancouver, Washington, in the United States. Vancouver's maps were used by all nineteenth-century mariners sailing from present-day Oregon to the Aleutians, and they were consulted during the Oregon Treaty negotiations in 1846. Despite the accuracy of his maps, Vancouver failed to discover the North West Passage and he said that it did not exist. The attacker was the nephew of the Prime Minister (William Pitt the Younger). He was also related to the First Lord of the Admiralty, John Pitt, and a brother of Lady Grenville, wife of the Foreign Secretary. The dispute was ostensibly about Vancouver's failure to accept Lord Camelford's challenge to a duel over alleged mistreatment of the aristocrat while he served on Vancouver's ship. In response to Camelford's letter requesting a duel, Vancouver replied that he was unable 'In a private capacity to answer for his public conduct in his official duty' and

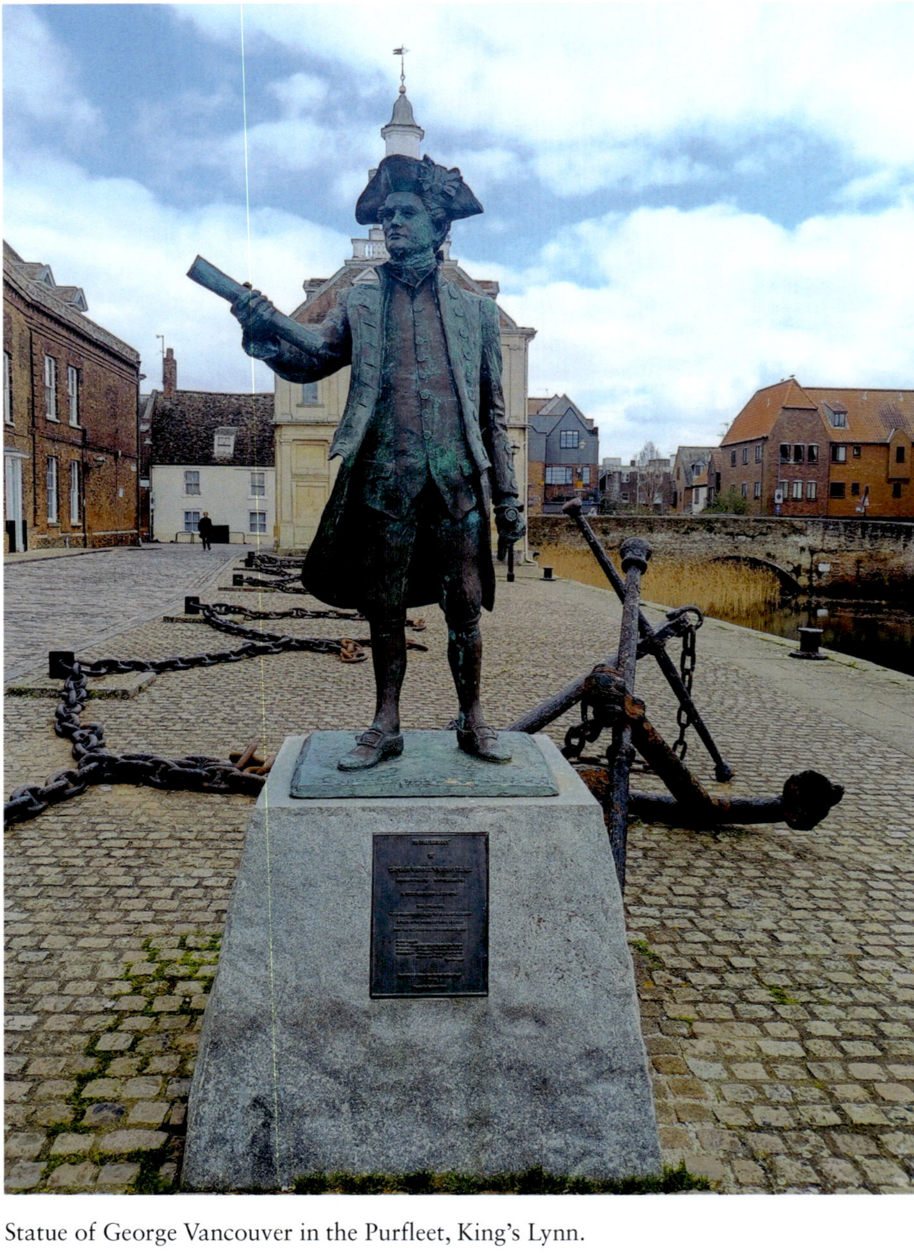

Statue of George Vancouver in the Purfleet, King's Lynn.

offered instead to submit to formal examination by flag officers. In 1791 when Vancouver sailed on his Pacific exploration expedition aboard HMS *Discovery* and HMS *Chatham,* Thomas Pitt was appointed to board *Chatham*. He was sixteen years old and very troublesome. Vancouver had him flogged three times for insubordination and put him ashore on Hawaii.

The most common punishment in the Royal Navy was flogging, and most sailors in the eighteenth and nineteenth centuries would likely have been flogged at least once during their time at sea. For minor infractions, or to punish young boys, caning with a rattan or birch cane was used. The usual instrument used to administer a flogging was the notorious cat o' nine tails, a whip made of nine strands of knotted rope (which were sometimes waxed, to maximize its brutal impact) tied together. The offender's shirt would be removed, and he would be tied to a secure part of the ship in preparation for the flogging. Each blow of the cat would open up numerous wounds, enough of which could prove fatal, on the unfortunate sailor's back. In the early days of the Royal Navy, flogging sentences were handed out for anything from drunkenness and insolence to neglect of duty or minor theft. The starting amount, for minor infractions, was usually a dozen lashes, but for serious offences this could go all the way up to thirty-six strokes. By 1750 a rule had been introduced that limited floggings to a maximum of twelve strokes. However, some captains got around this by dividing men's crimes into separate infractions, each of which could earn twelve lashes. For an especially severe infraction, the offender could be 'flogged around the fleet'. Once the naval ship reached a British port, the offender would be tied to the mast of a small boat, which would then visit every other naval ship in the harbour. A representative from each ship would deliver a number of lashes to the man with a cat o' nine tails, and the total number of lashes could end up being in the hundreds, if the punishment was taken to its extreme conclusion. Such a punishment was likely to be fatal. However, one seaman who apparently deserted and was captured, then 'flogged around the fleet', went on to become an admiral. He was Sir William Mitchell KCB (*c.* 1745–1816). This claim, which has never been backed up by firm evidence, may be accurate given the odd disappearance of Mitchell from Navy records between 1768 and 1777.

Thomas Pitt had been later discharged from another ship and involved in many drunken disputes and duels. In 1797 he refused to obey his commanding officer, Charles Peterson, and shot him dead. Camelford was court-martialled for this, but was later acquitted. In 1804 he died in a duel at the age of twenty-nine. Lord Camelford clearly resented being disciplined by the lowborn Vancouver. However, despite Camelford's behaviour before death, his family connections meant that it would have been very difficult for Vancouver ever to successfully defend a case against him. The Prime Minister had already verbally attacked the captain. When a full-length biography of Thomas Pitt was published in 1978, author Nikolai Tolstoy gave it the title '*The Half-Mad Lord*'.

Ghosts, Ghouls, Devils and Witches

Ghosts and Ghouls

Duke's Head Hotel

The Duke's Head Hotel was built in 1683 for a King's Lynn Member of Parliament, John Turner, and is attributed to Henry Bell, who designed and built many buildings in King's Lynn and Norfolk including the Customs House in King's Lynn. Bell (1647–1711) was an English architect, a contemporary of Christopher Wren. It is a four-star hotel and has been a Grade II listed building since 1 December 1951.The hotel stands on the site of an ancient inn called the 'Gryffin', which was demolished in 1683. A staircase in the present hotel was constructed from timbers reputedly from one of ships taken by Captain Vancouver on his voyages of discovery along the north-western coastline of North America. The frontage of the hotel was restored in the twentieth century. The building is reputed to be one of the most haunted buildings in this historic town.

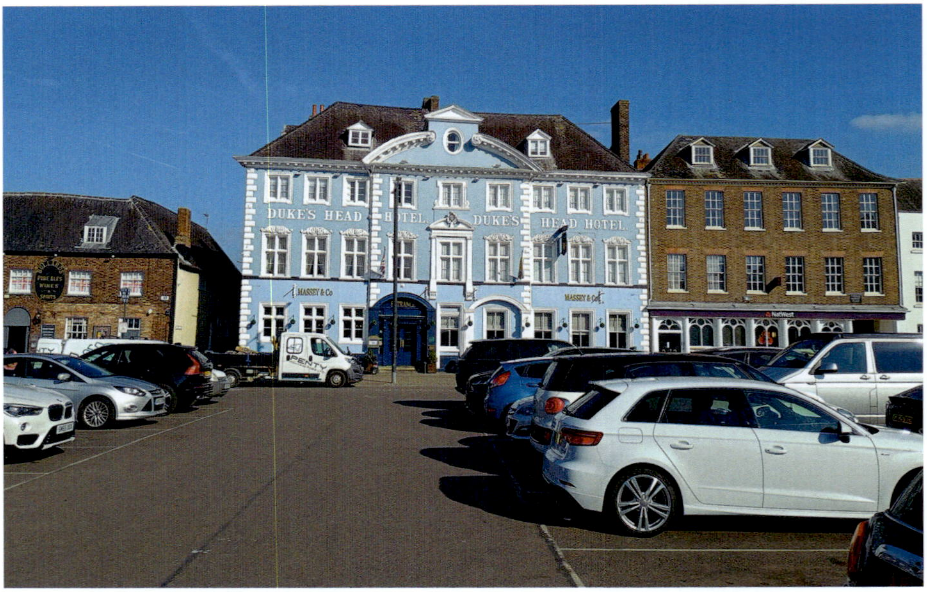

Duke's Head. This building is reputed to be one of the most haunted places in the historic town.

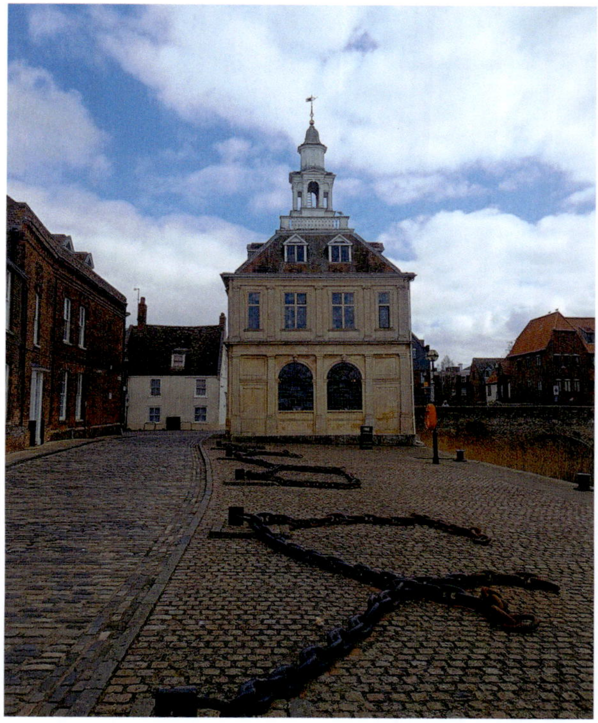

Grade I listed Customs House, Purfleet Quay, built in 1683 to the designs of Henry Bell.

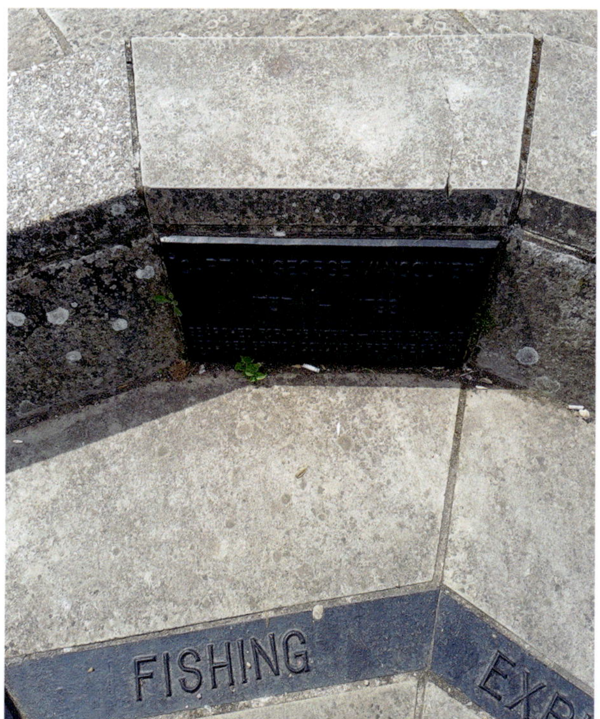

On the Purfleet Quay there is a compass rose with plaques commemorating eight significant people with links to King's Lynn. This honours Captain Vancouver.

The ghost of a maidservant is believed to roam the local landmark. According to reports, the maid was found guilty of poisoning her mistress and was sentenced to be boiled alive on the Tuesday Market Place. Dark discoveries have been found in the hotel. In 2011, cat remains were found in the ceiling of room ten. It is believed that the remains were placed there to deter evil spirits and witches entering the property as this was a popular method in England during the seventeenth century. A figure in red has been seen walking the corridors and climbing staircases. She is said to be the ghost of a woman who killed herself over her two lovers. Room eighteen was once haunted after an attempted suicide resulted in a dying man being brought into the suite, his ghostly moaning once drove people away, though now it has faded. That said, the hotel has undergone a full refurbishment programme with over 3£ million being spent. The bedrooms were decorated to a high standard with amenities including flat-screen TVs with over 100 channels, tea and coffee making facilities, en suites with power shower and free Wi-Fi. After all this work, the author hopes the ghosts of the past will have moved on.

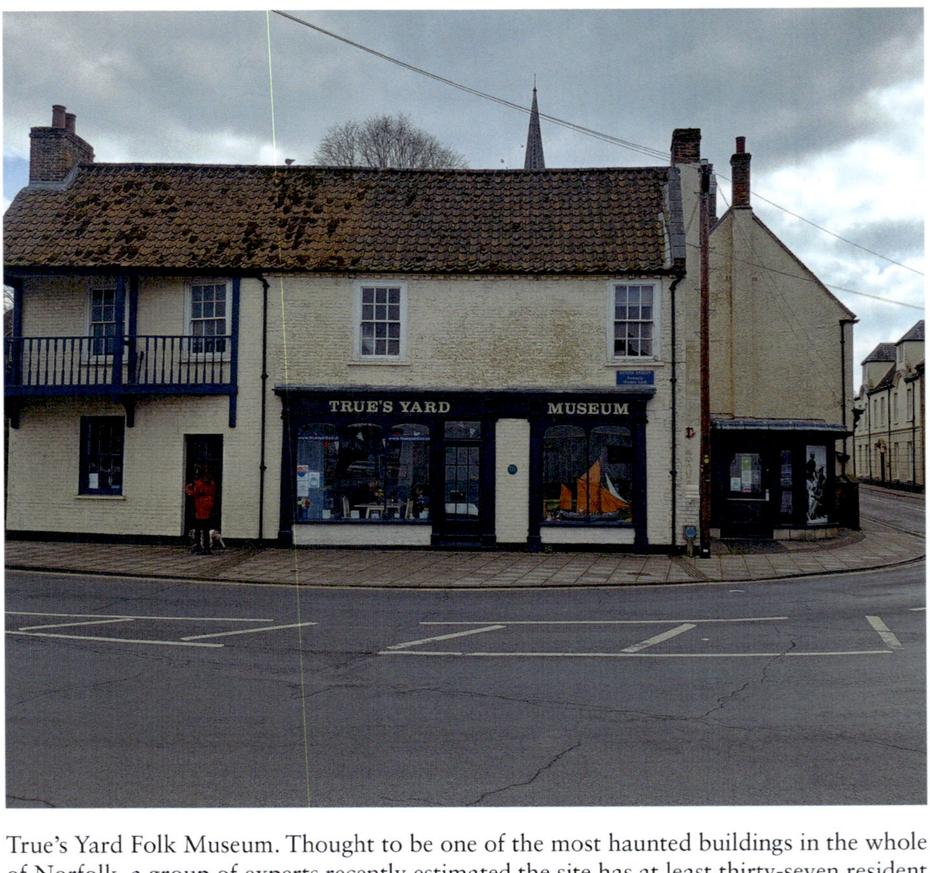

True's Yard Folk Museum. Thought to be one of the most haunted buildings in the whole of Norfolk, a group of experts recently estimated the site has at least thirty-seven resident ghosts.

True's Yard

True's Yard Fisherfolk Museum is a heritage site in the heart of King's Lynn celebrating the fishing community which once dominated the town's North End. The museum is made up of many different old buildings. There are other things besides history hidden in the museum's lovingly restored eighteenth-century cottages. True's Yard is thought to be one of the most haunted buildings in the whole of Norfolk; a group of experts recently estimated the site has at least thirty-seven resident ghosts. From spine-chilling sightings to unexplainable occurrences, there never seems to be a dull moment at True's Yard. Visitors have reported seeing spectral children waiting for their fisherman fathers, who had sacrificed their lives on the job, to return; disembodied voices and spirit orbs; mysterious shadows; and a dark figure looking out of an empty cottage window. The buildings also host the spirit of a man who was found hanging in the attic area of the museum. One part of the structure used to be an old pub and people have reported hearing groups of people in conversation there. It was also a recruitment place during the First World War and many of these recruits died, so it is thought that they returned to the pub as ghosts. Two separate visitors reported seeing the same figure sitting in a chair in one of the bedrooms, a young woman with bulging red eyes and red marks on her throat. This could be the spirit of a woman who was strangled by her father for loving the wrong man. As well as chills and spooky figures, True's Yard is home to mischievous spirits with an appetite for causing chaos. A troublesome poltergeist affectionately known as Henry resides in a room where fisherfolk used to live and is thought to be responsible for paintings getting knocked off walls, bulbs regularly blowing and staplers flying across the room. Staff have also reported a ghostly boy in the museum's kitchen who enjoys moving things about.

Tudor Rose Hotel

The former Tudor Rose Hotel has stood just off the Tuesday Market Place on St Nicholas Street since the fifteenth century, when it was built on the site of a former nunnery and surrounded by the town's old defensive walls. The building was said to be haunted by a woman in a long white dress, who is believed to be the ghost of a bride stabbed to death by her husband on her wedding day in the hotel and who was seen in room seven, while her footsteps had been heard elsewhere in the building. Sometimes a strange figure clearing the snow from the yard at Christmas was observed. Regularly shadows passed and items were moved, doors opened by themselves, and a cold chill stole into certain rooms. A Grey Lady also appeared and was seen in the hotel restaurant. The hotel closed in 2017 and then became residential dwellings. I am unaware of any further reported manifestations since the conversion. It is to be hoped they are all now at peace.

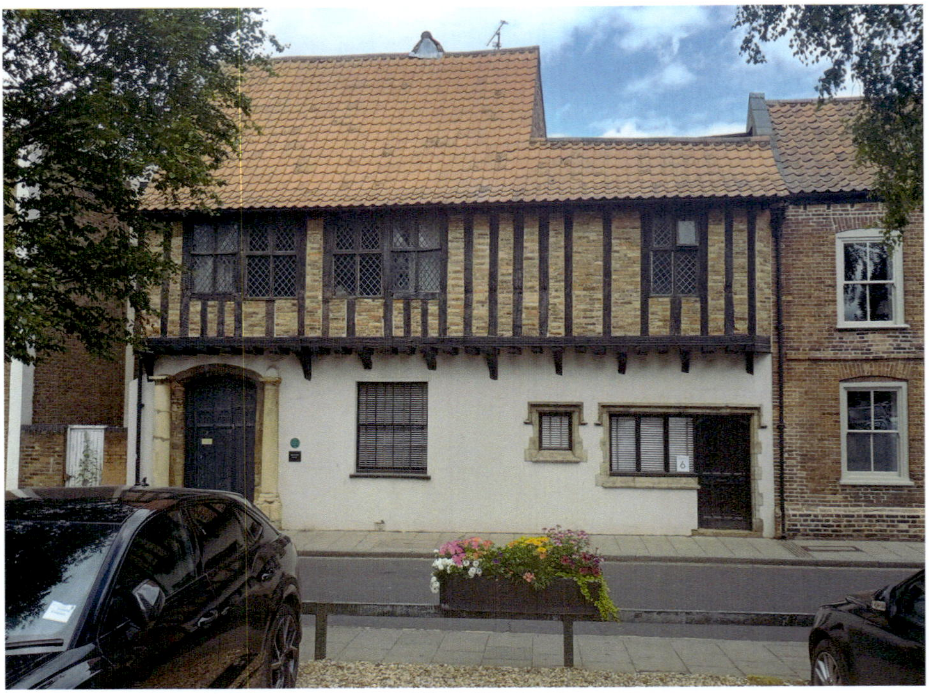

Former Tudor Rose Hotel, now residential dwellings and a B&B. I am unaware of any further reported manifestations since the conversion. It is to be hoped that they are now at peace.

Nos 28–32 King Street

Metcalfe Copeman and Pettefar LLP (MCP), based in what is probably Lynn's oldest townhouse, were established in 1784 and have been in continuous practice ever since. The building includes the remains of the earliest known domestic building in King's Lynn dating from as far back as the twelfth century. Even the modern parts of the building are almost 500 years old, and it may well be the oldest office building in the entire country. Acquired and restored by the King's Lynn Preservation Trust in the late 1970s, it is normally open to the public on Heritage Open Day and strictly by appointment. Staff at this historic solicitors' office are used to bumps and creaks in the night while working late. But spectral piano playing, ghostly New Year festivities and the apparition of a young man in a military trench coat made several of them more than a little wary of burning the midnight oil. In 1996, a secretary, who did not wish to be named, said she had heard footsteps while working late and felt she was being watched. She saw the young man in the trench coat but when she said 'Hello', he disappeared.

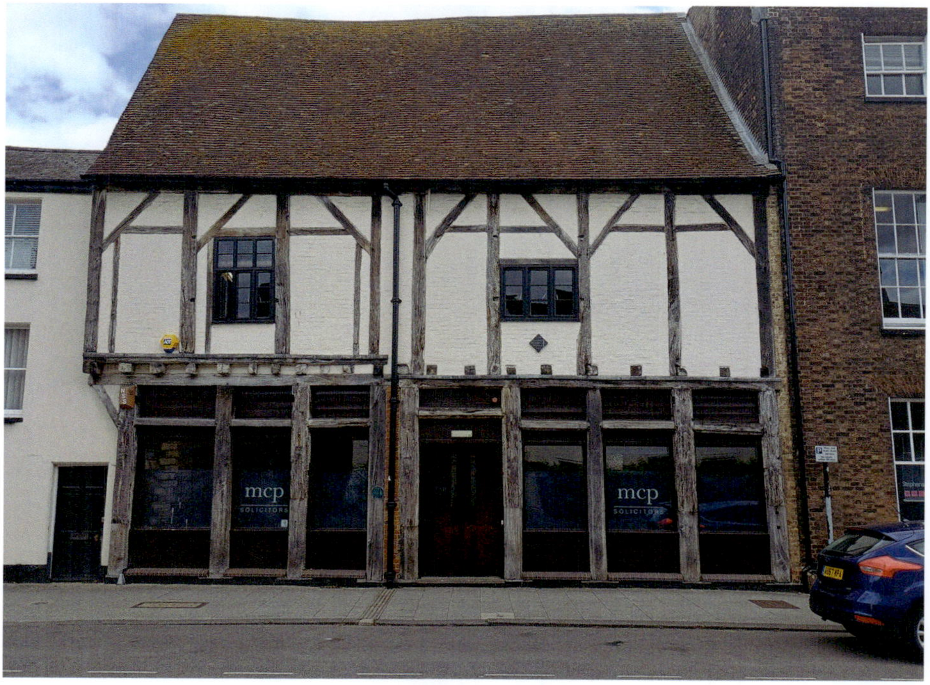

Nos 28–32 King Street. One of the most interesting houses in Lynn and the oldest office building in the entire country.

No. 9 King Street

In the 1970s, the ghost of an eighteenth-century gentleman was seen by several different people in this building. The site of a medieval merchant's house, one visitor to the building, when it was a museum, spotted a man in a tricorn hat. walking around with his hands behind his back.

Purfleet Quay

The Purfleet Quay was King's Lynn's principal anchorage for ships during medieval times. A ghost is said to loiter in the area, before screaming and throwing herself into the quay. She is said to be a woman who killed herself the day after she was married. Other ghostly screams in the area are attributed to fighting soldiers, and if these screams are heard, the water is said to run red with blood.

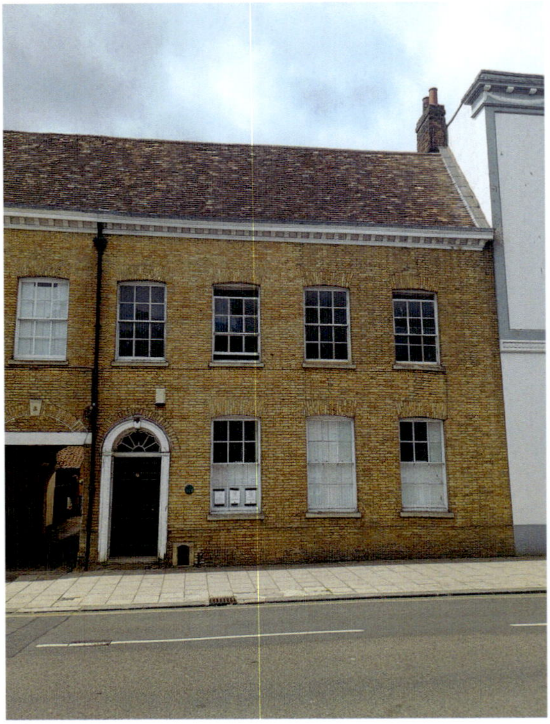

No. 9 King Street is haunted by a man in a three-cornered hat.

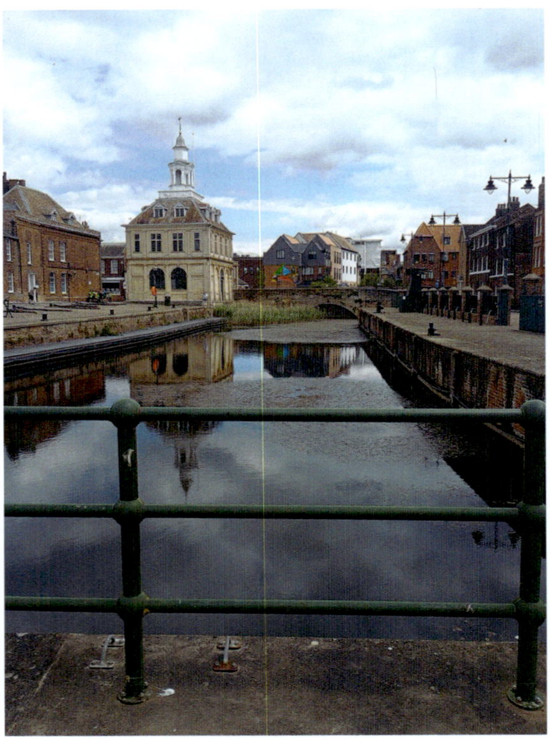

Purfleet Quay. Scene of many hauntings and manifestations.

Devils

Devil's Alley

Legend has it that Mephistopheles arrived in Lynn by ship and went ashore to gather some souls. He was then, fortunately, spotted by a priest who cornered him in what is now known as 'Devil's Alley', banishing him back to the netherworld with prayers and holy water. The infuriated devil stamped his foot in fury and

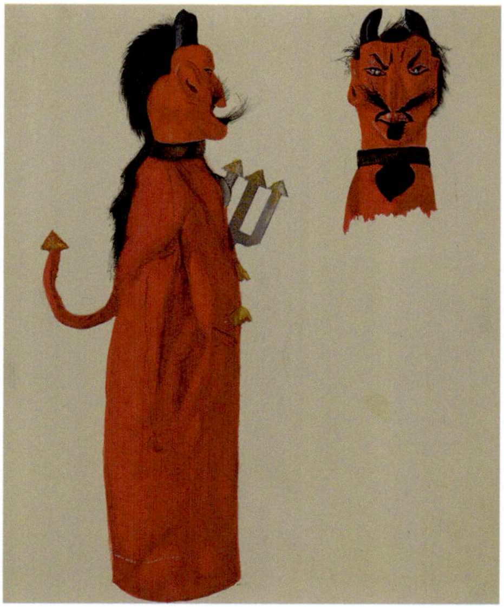

Mephistopheles. The least threatening illustration I could find. *Hand Puppet-Devil*, Joseph Shapiro, *c.* 1936. (National Gallery of Art)

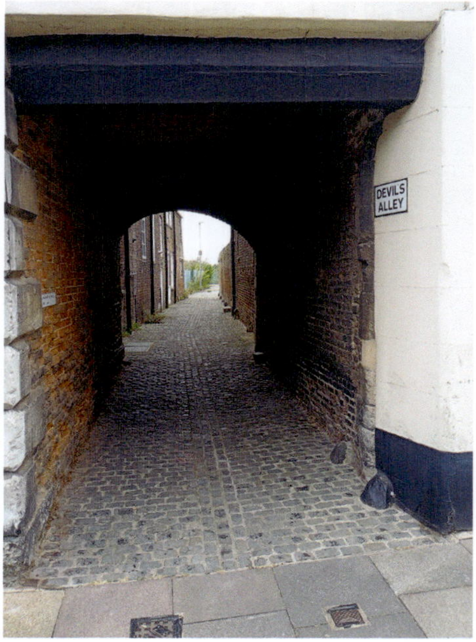

Devil's Alley. In 1881, the alley was called Millers Alley.

with such force that it left an imprint and acted as a reminder of the chaos he could wreak. 'Devil's Alley' was once completely roofed like a tunnel and ran all the way to the quayside. It is said that rather than an imprint in the ground, the alley showed at its darkest point a queer cobble in the pavement shaped like a gigantic human foot. One would think that the Devil has cloven hoofs not feet but not having met the gentleman, at least in his recognised form, I cannot comment further. While the alley remains, the footprint has long since disappeared, a victim of modern roadworks which have seen the cobbles resurfaced. But one mystery remains: in 1881, the alley was called 'Miller's, not 'Devil's Alley'. Lucifer may have therefore made a relatively recent return visit to the town. In January 2025, regeneration ideas for 'Devil's Alley' were revealed by the local council with the local community consulted to shape a better and more ambitious design. There was a somewhat vain hope that the footprint would be reinstated, although with the appropriate deterrent measures taken to stop a repeat visit. However, in February 2025, the plans were withdrawn due to an angry flood of objections for people living on nearby Nelson Street.

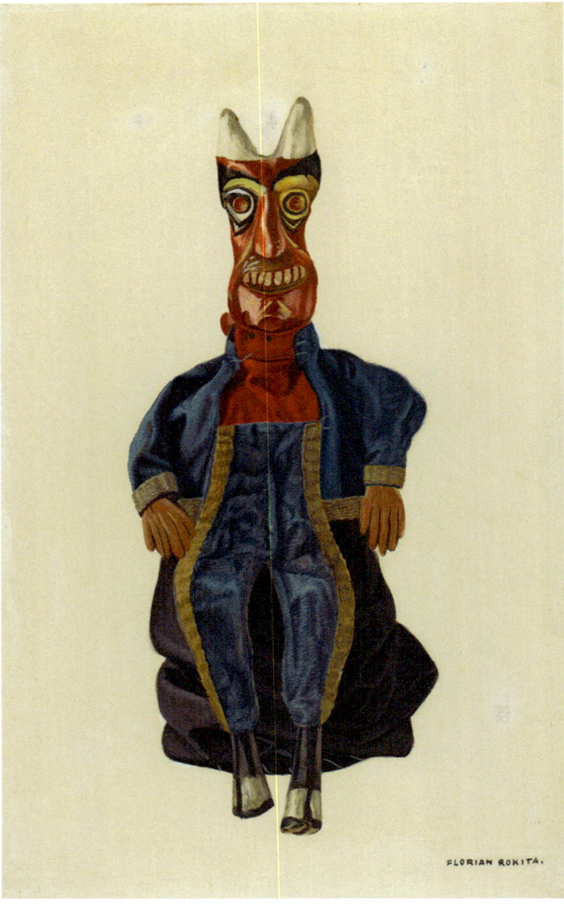

Lucifer, a very dapper devil. *Old Nick, the Devil*, Florian Rokita, *c*. 1936. (National Gallery of Art)

Deucehill

At the east end of St Nicholas' Chapel runs Pilot Street. Before 1809 it was known as 'Dowshill'. In the Middle Ages it was spelt 'Deucehill, Douz Hill' and 'Duse Hill'. 'Duse' is an old word used to describe demons or the Devil, so it has been suggested that this area was a known haunt of Old Nick, fiends and goblins. The Devil was all too real back in those days, people believed he was a physical entity

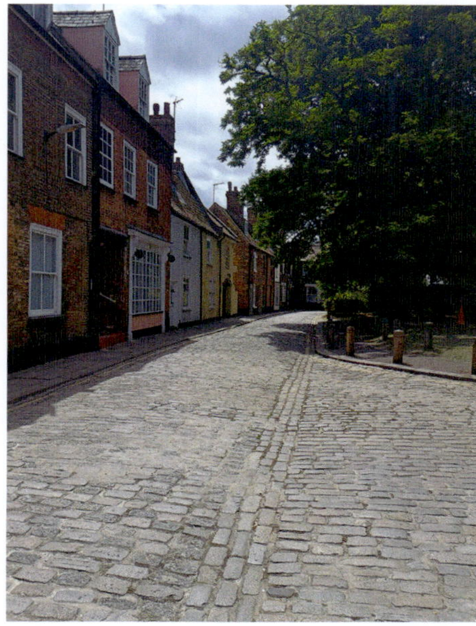

Peaceful, tranquil Pilot Street today. Home to at least ten pubs over the years.

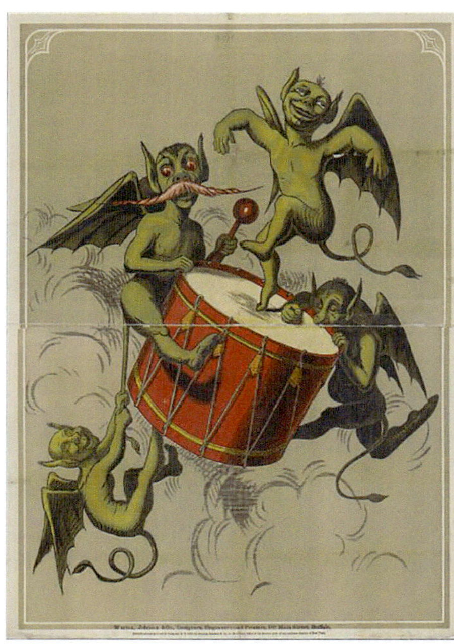

Devilish figures beating a drum, circus poster, *c.* 1870. (Library of Congress)

who chased souls and with whom certain people, witches, could communicate. A saying of ancient origin, 'Deuce' is also practically synonymous with the devil, the word being derived from 'Dusins', the ancient name given by the Gauls to a sort of demon or devil. The expression 'what the deuce' is a current use of the word as a milder type of oath. At one time this little street was home to at least ten public houses, all of which have now disappeared. This may possibly explain some of the supernatural sightings but this cannot be confirmed.

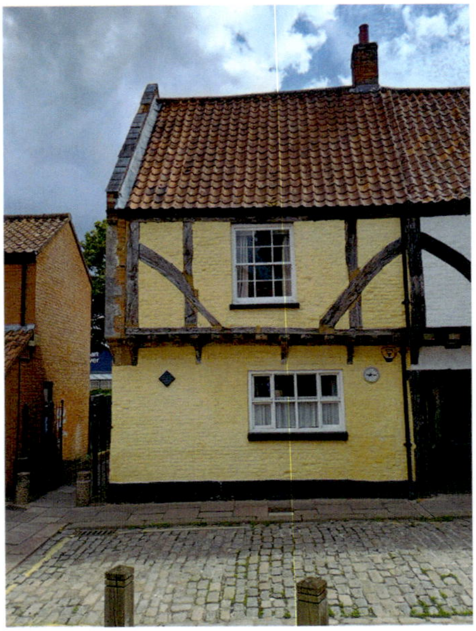

Former Grampus pub in Pilot Street, closed in 1921. A Grampus is a widely distributed dolphin.

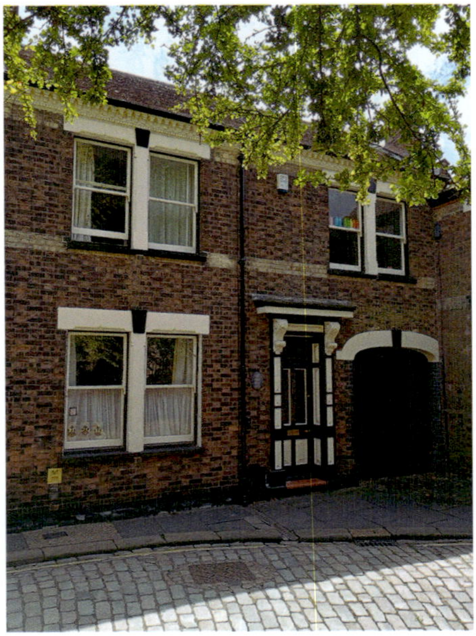

Another former pub, The Pilot Hoy, closed in 1906. Hoy means 'a decked vessel', commonly rigged as a sloop.

Witches

In the days before rational medical and scientific knowledge the practice of witchcraft was a common belief. The frenzy for witch hunting really began in the reign of James I, who apparently came into contact with it in Germany, but fear of witches had been rife for decades before then, as witness the legend of the witch's heart at No. 17 Tuesday Market Place. The Market Place had long

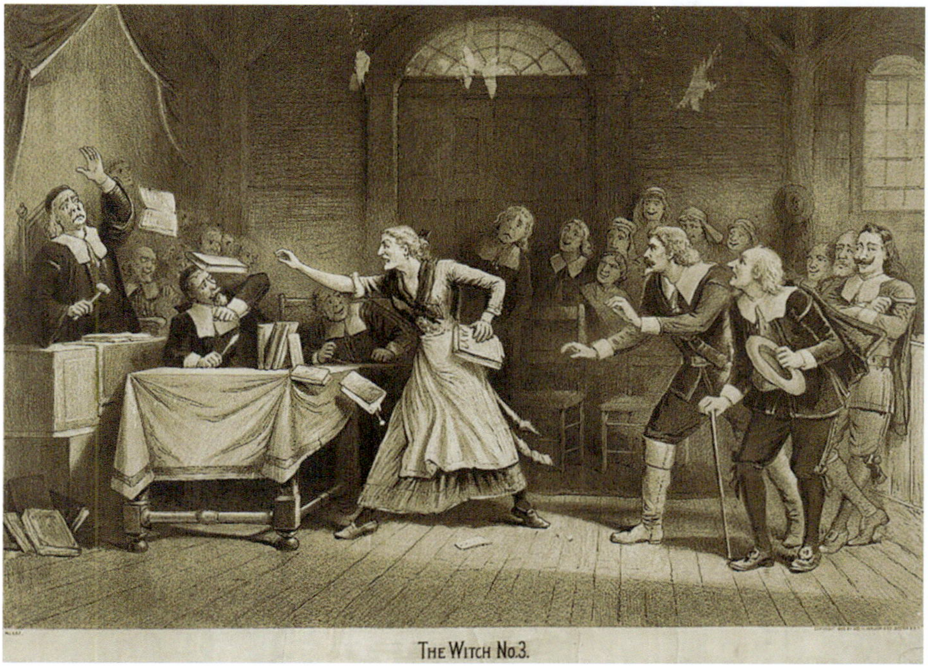

Above: Witch fighting back at the jury, Geo. Walker & Co., *c.* 1892. (Library of Congress)

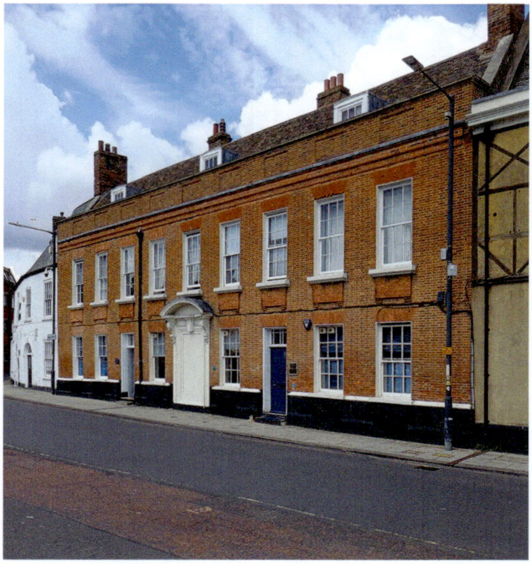

Right: No. 17 Tuesday Market Place, the site of the legend of the witch's heart.

been a place for public execution, and the story goes that one witch who was burned alive in 1590 was named Margaret Read. At the moment of death, her heart burst from her body, struck the wall, leaving the mark still to be seen today. It then, with an energy all its own, bounced its way to the river, presumably via Page Stair Street, and plunged into the water, causing it to froth and boil. Other

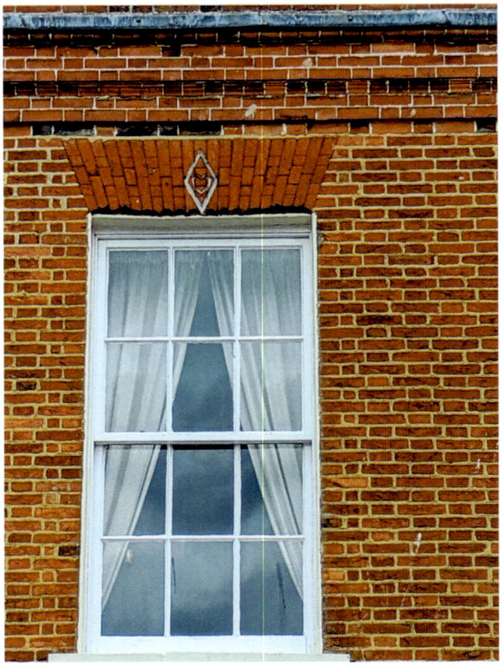

Mark of the burst heart. Perhaps not as awesome as you might have hoped.

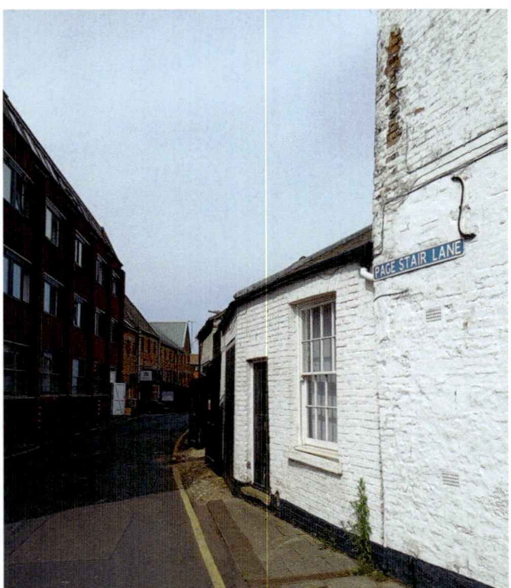

Page Stair Street. No evidence of any burst heart remains and it no longer leads to the river.

executions included Mary Smith, burnt in 1616, Dorothy Lee and Grace Wright, hanged in 1646, and Dorothy Floyd, or Lloyd, in 1650. Mother Gabley was the first person condemned in Norfolk under the 1563 Act Against Conjurations, Enchantments and Witchcrafts, which was passed early in the reign of Elizabeth I. She was accused of causing the death of Robert Archer, Oliver Cobb, William Barret, Henry Gouldsmith, Richard Dye and others who had sailed from Spain to England. In all, thirteen men had died. She had, it was claimed, boiled eggs in water, stirring vigorously to raise a storm at sea. Mother Gabley was hanged in King's Lynn in 1583, probably at Tuesday Market Place. The burning of witches was surprisingly rare in England, although this was a common punishment in Scotland and mainland Europe. Part of the reason behind this was the cost of burning. In 1645, it cost £3 3*s* 6*d* to burn a witch, compared to £1 to hang her. That's around £433 in 2025 for burning, rather than £136 for hanging.

In 1646 Matthew Hopkins was asked to clear King's Lynn of witches. The town leaders agreed to pay £15, although that was later upped to £17. He had previously been £23 for clearing Chelmsford. The average worker was only earning two and a half pence a day. Hopkins was born in Suffolk at the beginning of the seventeenth century. Some people think he was trained as a lawyer because of the way he presented his evidence in court. He called himself the 'Witchfinder General', although that title was never given to him by parliament, and he was not a man to let truth get in the way of good public relations. He operated mainly in Suffolk, Essex, Norfolk, Cambridgeshire and Huntingdonshire, with a few visits in the counties of Northamptonshire and Bedfordshire. Hopkins began his career in March 1644 when he allegedly first discovers six witches in Manningtree, claiming they tried to kill him. He soon toured about East Anglia getting people to hire him to hunt out witches, force their confessions, and have them hanged by the authorities. The Church of England's break from Catholicism in the previous century led to religious fragmentation and increased suspicion towards individuals seen as Nonconformists. Puritans, seeking a pure society, emphasised the battle between good and evil, often identifying witches as agents of the devil. This attitude fuelled witch hunts, particularly during the English Civil War when Puritan authority was strong. Hopkins was a sincere, zealous Protestant, but he exploited local anxieties about purity and morality. He is believed to have been responsible for the executions of over one hundred alleged witches between the years 1644 and 1646. He and his colleague, John Stearne, sent more accused people to the gallows than all the other witch hunters in England in the previous 160 years. Hopkins died in 1647 of tuberculosis and was buried on 12 August in Manningtree. However, before his death he published his book *The Discovery of Witches*. This led to witch hunting in the New England Colonies, which lasted until 1663, and some of his methods were used in the Salem Witch Trials of 1692–93.

Three Unconventional Figures from the Past

Nicholas of Lynn

Nicholas of Lynn or Lynne, also known in Latin as Nicolas de Linna, was an English astronomer of the fourteenth century. The plaque on the Greyfriars Tower in the town may not be strictly accurate in some respects. There is another plaque in the Compass Rose at Purfleet Quay with plaques commemorating eight significant people with links to King's Lynn. This is even more inaccurate if modern research is correct. He was apparently born in the port town of Bishop's Lynn, now King's Lynn, possibly as early as 1330, although the confirmed details of his career suggest that a date closer to 1360 is more likely. According to early

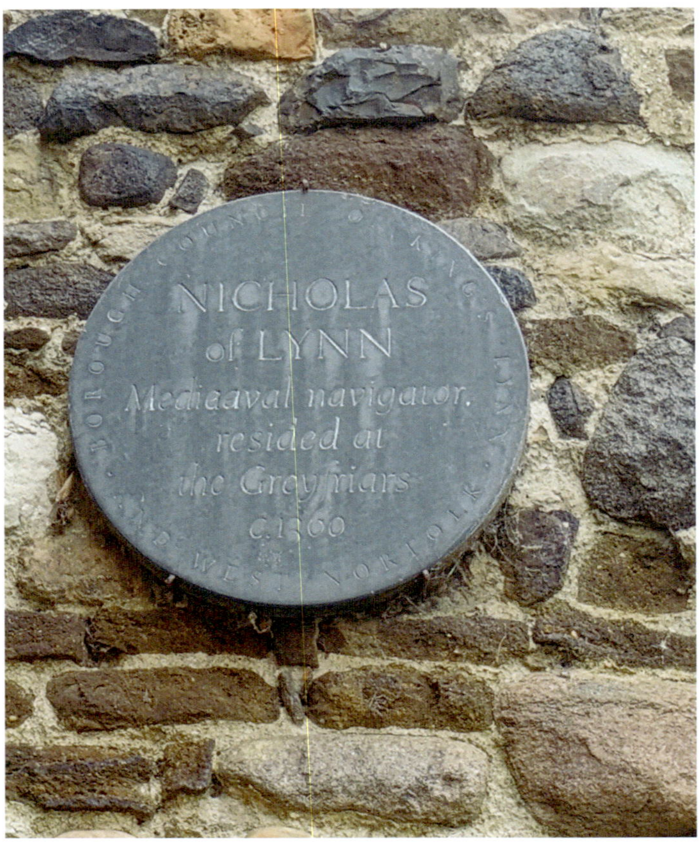

Possibly misleading plaque at Greyfriars Tower.

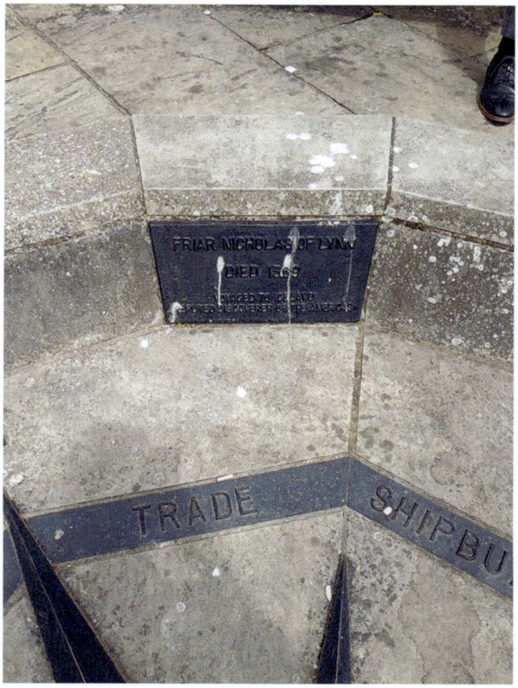

Another inaccurate plaque at Purfleet Quay following modern research.

sixteenth century literary historian John Bale, he became a Carmelite friar and moved to the university town of Oxford, where he developed a great reputation for his scientific work. In 1386, at the request of the powerful lord John of Gaunt, one of Edward III's sons, he published a '*Kalendarium*' of detailed astronomical tables covering the years 1387–1462. It survives in sixteen manuscripts and one printed edition and is available to purchase online. Designed for use in the astrologically based science of the time, the tables were very sophisticated, even including rules for synchronising medical treatment with astronomical cycles, such as the right phases of the moon for bloodletting. His contemporary Geoffrey Chaucer wrote very approvingly of Nicholas' work, and made much use of it. He refers to the friar as 'that reverend clerk, frere Nicholas de Lenn'.

Nicholas was also supposedly an excellent musician. Later in life he moved to Cambridge, where he was promoted to subdeacon in 1410 and to deacon in 1411. What he was not, as far as any early biographers were concerned, was an explorer. It is only in recent years, however, that Nicholas of Lynne has acquired a considerable reputation as an early English explorer of the Arctic, in spite of the absurdity of the statements that he travelled alone to the North Pole and later made five further Arctic expeditions. These claims that Nicholas was the Franciscan who voyaged to Iceland and reputedly discovered the Americas are now very much questioned. Thomas Blundeville seems to have come nearer to the truth when he wrote in 1589 that he did not believe that the friar had made a voyage to the Arctic 'unlesse he had some colde Devill out of the middle Region of the aire to be his guide'.

The identification of Nicholas as the Franciscan friar who wrote a text called the *Inventio Fortunata*, allegedly describing a voyage to Greenland and beyond, was first proposed by Richard Hakluyt, the late sixteenth-century historian of exploration. Hakluyt based the claim on information from mathematician John Dee who, in turn, relied on information obtained from the Dutch cartographer Gerardus Mercator.

John Dee (1527–1608/9) was an English scholar who wrote on trigonometry, calendar reform, navigation, geography and astrology. He became astrologer to Queen Mary but was imprisoned for being a magician. Nicholas, however, was a Carmelite, not a Minorite, and if Hakluyt and Dee had read Bale, they would have discovered an entry about a Franciscan friar named Hugh of Ireland, who wrote 'a certain journey in one volume'. As late as the seventeenth century, Henry Hudson used the book when he set off to explore the Arctic, and it seems that the volume did indeed, give a pretty accurate description of North East Canada and Greenland. It is thought that Columbus himself might have also had a copy. Some think the author may have met someone else who had travelled north, and transcribed these experiences as if he himself had been the voyager. A recent novel, *Far Faring for Falcons: An Arctic Voyage with Nicholas of Lynn* by Spencer Apollonio invents a scenario in which gyrfalcons in the fourteenth century were rare and very valuable. The largest falcon in the world, the ghostly Gyrfalcon, is a fierce predator in the High Arctic, where it chases down ptarmigans, a grouse that typically changes to white in winter, in flight or plummets from the sky at breathtaking speeds to strike prey to the ground. The narrator is compelled to seek and capture them in the Arctic because royalty in Egypt holds his brother in ransom. His quest is imperilled by the Hundred Years' War, the bubonic plague, and the rival ruler of Damascus. Nicholas of Lynn, invites him on a voyage to the Arctic but officials in Greenland try to stop the quest for falcons. The three-year quest leads them to spend a year with native people, the northernmost in the world, from whom they develop new perspectives on European society and civilization.

Joe Dines

Today's stereotyped conventional image of a professional footballer is, perhaps, a heavily tattooed young man driving an Italian sports car between nightclubs, with a dizzy blonde in the passenger seat. Early last century nothing could be further from the truth. Some players even turned down the chance to become professionally paid sportsmen. Born on 12 April 1886, Joseph Dines was the youngest of four sons of Frank and Josephine Dines of No. 4 Whitefriars Terrace. His early football was with Lynn All Saints and then Lynn United playing for the latter's second team in the 1902/03 season before being 'poached' by Lynn Town.

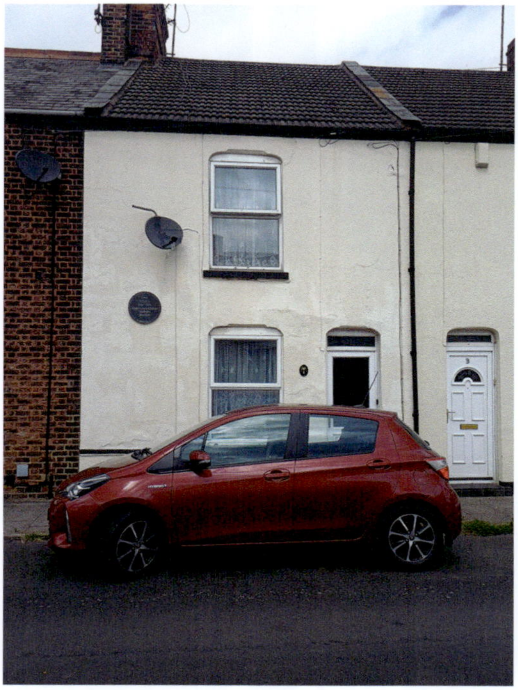

The terraced home in an unassuming street which produced 'The Smiling Footballer'.

He started in Lynn Reserves and then went on to make his first team debut on 13 February 1904 against Peterborough Loco in the Dereham Charity Cup. He then became a Lynn regular, taking part in Lynn's FA Cup encounter with Aston Villa in 1906 and receiving his county colours that season. He was also in the Norfolk team that won the Southern Counties Championship in 1908 and made appearances for Norwich Reserves and Woolwich Arsenal Reserves. He trained as a teacher in Peterborough and returned to Lynn, becoming an assistant master at St Margaret's. He moved to Ilford Football Club in 1910, by which time he had already started on an international career that was to lead to twenty-four caps with England's amateurs and had played for Queen's Park Rangers. At the time Ilford were a renowned amateur team playing, ironically, at Lynn Road, Ilford. He was much loved by Ilford's regular supporters. He lived at No. 5 Toronto Road, by Valentines Park, and was a dedicated teacher to the pupils of Highlands School for three years. It was in the 1912 Stockholm Olympics that Joe Dines played in all three games for the Great Britain & Northern Ireland team as they retained the gold medal won in 1908 with victories over Hungary 7-0, Finland 4-0 and Denmark 4-2 in the final on 4 July. Resisting attempts to persuade him to become professional, he appeared occasionally for clubs such as Walthamstow Avenue, Millwall and even one appearance for Liverpool when they visited Chelsea, Liverpool winning 2-1. He is also reported as still making the occasional appearance for Lynn as late as the 1913–14 season. He made 149 appearances for Lynn, scoring twenty-eight goals.

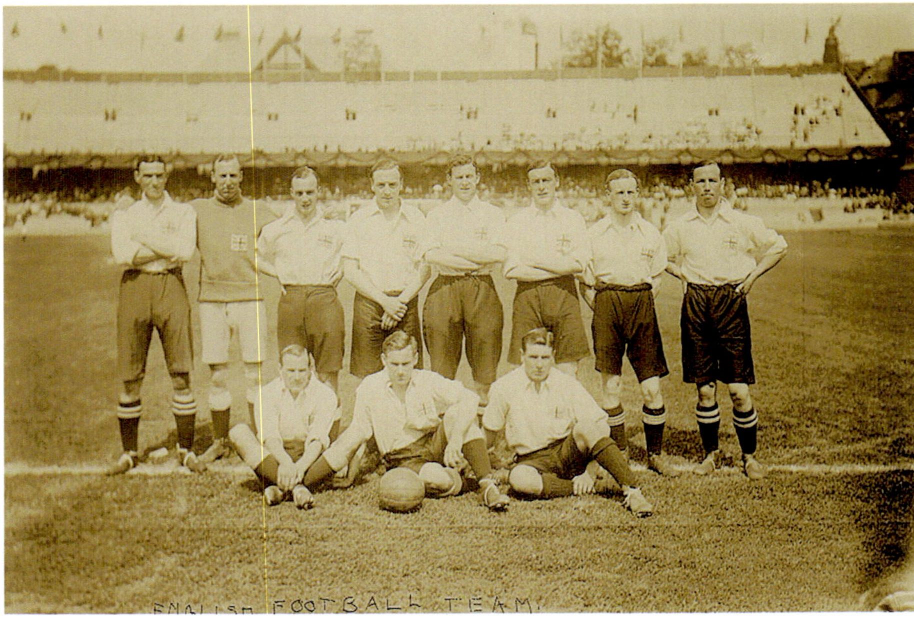

Great Britain's 1912 Olympic Football gold medallists. Joe Dines is back row left next to the goalkeeper. (Library of Congress)

Joe married King's Lynn-born Ethel Burgoyne in 1913, the daughter of a retired customs officer. Joe was one of three brothers to volunteer immediately on the outbreak of the First World War. He served with the Ordnance Corps, the Middlesex Regiment, the Machine Gun Corps and the Tank Corps, before being commissioned into the Liverpool regiment as a Second Lieutenant. He even played that one game for Liverpool FC before he was sent to France. Joe served for only eleven days on the Western Front before he was killed by a burst of machine gun fire in Pas de Calais on 27 September 1918. Joe had been leading an attack on an enemy position. The battalion took 600 prisoners but lost six officers and 125 men in the action. He is buried at Grand Ravine British Cemetery in Harvincourt, France. Often known as 'The Smiling Footballer', he was a thoughtful young man, a commanding half-back and 'master of the art of dribbling'. He was on leave in Lynn just three weeks before he met his death. He left a young widow, parents, siblings and many admirers. There is a plaque in his memory at Millwall Football Club. He is commemorated on the war memorial at All Saints, South Lynn and the King's Lynn war memorial. Family man, student, teacher, footballer, Olympian, soldier, commissioned officer and one of the fallen of the First World War, a man whose name is carved on numerous memorials and whose story is shared by many within and beyond King's Lynn. We should all remember Joe Dines.

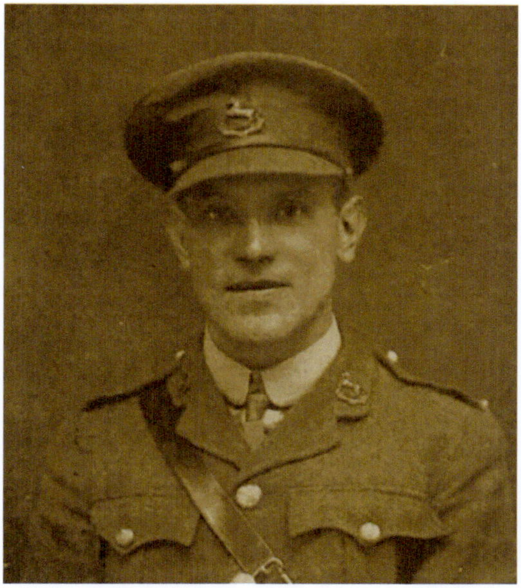

Joe Dines in uniform. (Find A Grave)

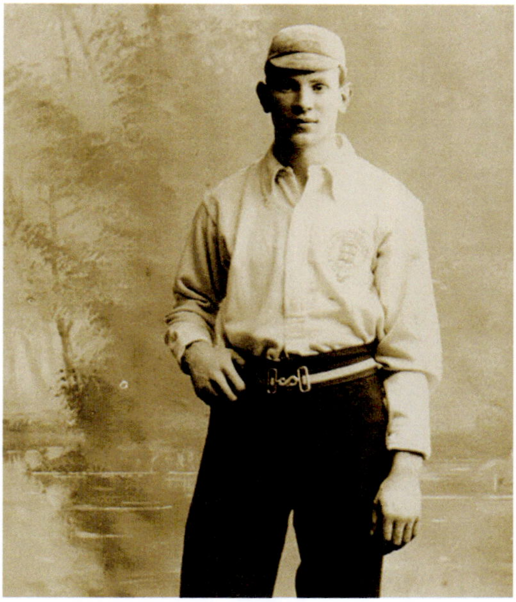

The Smiling Footballer. (Find A Grave)

Margery Kempe

Margery Kempe was a mystic, visionary and pilgrim. She was born around 1373, the daughter of a successful and influential Lynn merchant. Following her marriage and the birth of her first child, she had frequent visions of Christ and conversations with Our Lady and other saints. The church of St Margaret, St Mary Magdalene and All the Virgin Saints (today known as King's Lynn Minster) was her parish church. Margery came from a wealthy and influential

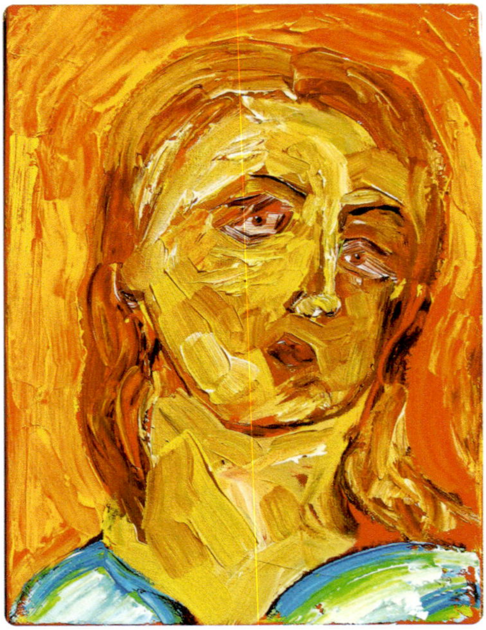

Margery Kempe, a modern interpretation in a painting. (By permission of Steve Hammond, Michigan, USA)

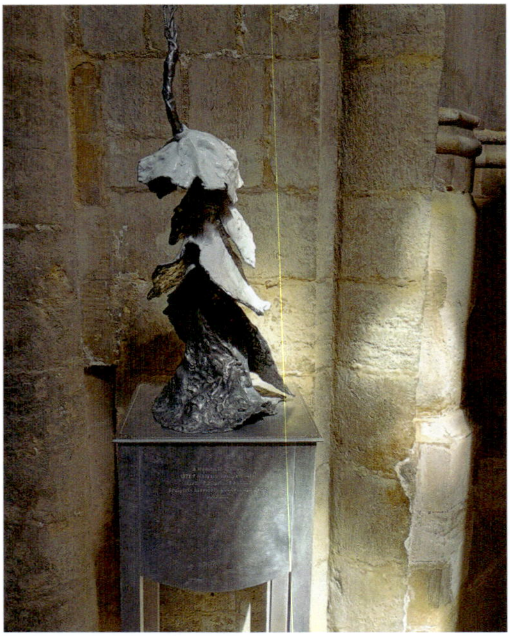

A Woman in Motion, a sculpture of Margery Kempe by Rosemary Goodenough in King's Lynn Minster, head bowed in prayer and dressed in swirling pilgrim attire.

family of merchants. Her father was John Brunham, five times mayor of Lynn, MP, and alderman of the Holy Trinity Guild. She married John Kempe, a burgess of Lynn, in 1393. Their marriage produced fourteen children, although it is unclear how many of them survived into adulthood. As a medieval woman from Bishop's Lynn, Margery was accustomed to a life of wealth as evident from her fashionable outfits, with gold pipes in her hair and slit dresses displaying colourful and expensive fabrics. To supplement her household income, she set up a brewing business and took to milling, but all her ventures eventually failed. Margery's first pregnancy resulted in a difficult birth and an episode of mental distress which many modern scholars have diagnosed as 'postpartum psychosis'. She was plagued by terrifying visions of demons and had to be restrained in her bedchamber so as to not cause harm to herself and others. The torments were all lifted when she saw a vision of Christ at her bedside, who spoke to her: 'Daughter, why have you forsaken me, and I never forsook you? '

This vision and the ones that followed caused a shift in Margery's life. She desired to dedicate her life to Christ and spent many hours at prayer in St Margaret's Church. She wore a hairshirt underneath her clothes and fasted on bread and water. She also desired chastity and pleaded with her husband that they should take a vow of abstinence together. One of the key manifestations of Margery's faith were her uncontrollable bouts of weeping. In the Church it was believed she had been granted the 'gift of tears'. Margery was moved to visit holy shrines so that she could understand God's message better. Her early pilgrimages were undertaken in the company of her husband. She travelled to shrines

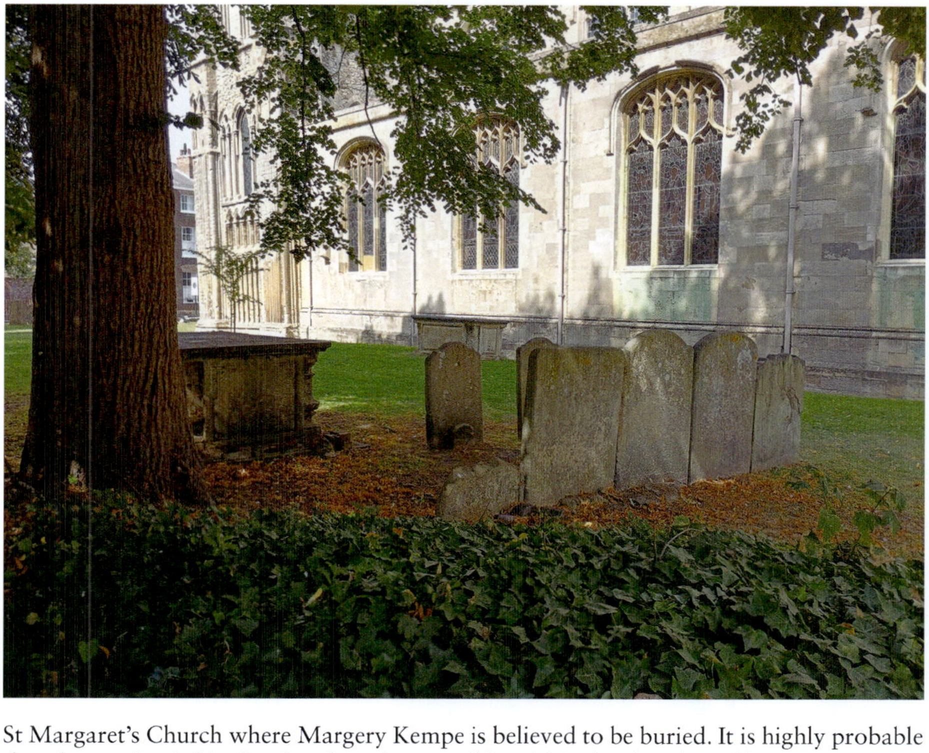

St Margaret's Church where Margery Kempe is believed to be buried. It is highly probable that she was buried in the churchyard or possibly within the church itself, as was common for the time, especially for someone of her status.

across England, often seeking validation for her visions and experiences. She visited Julian of Norwich in 1413 to seek her guidance and reassurance. Julian confirmed that Margery's visions came from God and that her tears are physical evidence of the Holy Spirit in her soul. Whilst she was generally welcomed on her travels abroad, including making pilgrimages to Jerusalem, Rome and Santiago di Compostela, in England she found many were against her.

The *Book of Margery Kempe* is known as the first spiritual autobiography in English. Margery claims she was illiterate and 'not lettryd', so she dictated her book to scribes. It is not a chronological account of her life, but a fascinating dialogue between Margery and visions of God, Christ and the saints, about faith and the meaning of a good Christian life. The book ignores anything that is not primarily the story of Margery's relationship with God and her spiritual journey. The purpose of her work is to reveal and authorise the meaning and truth she believes God had called her to follow. The book is divided into two parts. The first part in many ways follows the format of similar devotional texts of the period, particularly those by women mystics and visionaries. Through various experiences, childbirth, madness and her first vision of Christ, Margery narrates her spiritual journey, which leads to her travels, and the 'gift of tears'. Margery recalls accusations of Lollardy made against her, as well as her travels to the Holy Land, Assisi, Rome and Santiago di Compostela. She also details two great fires in Lynn. So concerned was she for her parish church that when one of the fires was destroying the nearby Hall of the Trinity Guild (1421) and threatened

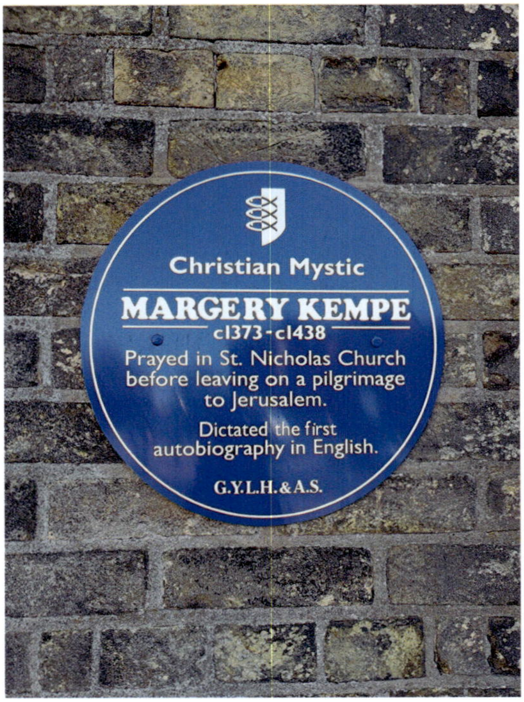

A plaque on the fence surrounding the Yarmouth Minster. In 1413 this was a stop on her way to Rotterdam, Bologna, Venice and then the Holy Land.

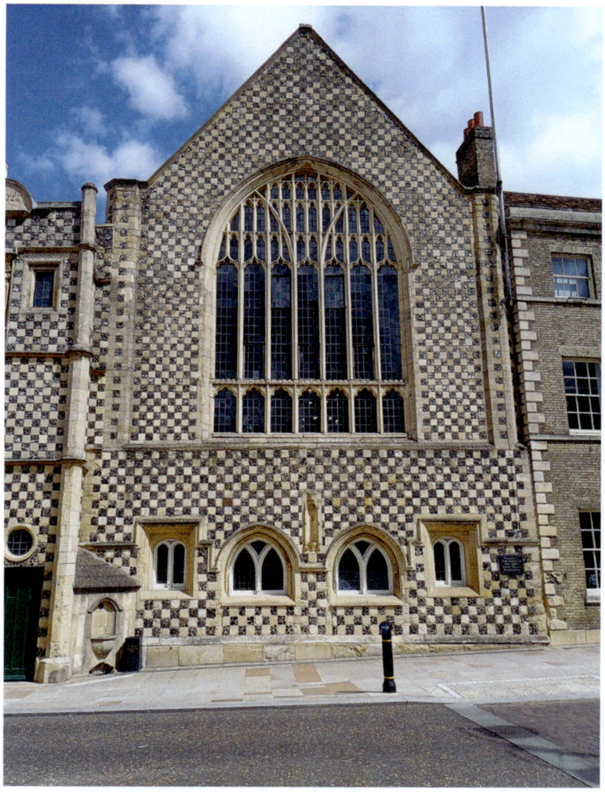

The Guildhall of St George is a Grade I listed building. It is the largest extant guildhall in England.

to burn down St Margaret's, she encouraged the parish priest to raise the Holy Sacrament (consecrated Host) before the fire as she prayed with loud weeping. Soon after, she gave praise to God when snow came down, miraculously dousing the conflagration.

The Guildhall has been in use as a theatre since 1445, making it the oldest theatre still operating in the United Kingdom and the only one still in existence in which William Shakespeare is believed to have performed. The second part resembles a travel journal, or memoir. It features the death of Margery's husband, John Kempe, as well as her son. Margery accompanies her daughter-in law back to Prussia and travels on to Danzig and Aachen, finally returning to Syon Abbey. It is clear from her book that Margery not only has an extremely retentive memory, but that she is very familiar with other books of devotion and spirituality, the Liturgy of the Church, as well as the Bible. Whilst Margery challenges bishops and ecclesiastical authorities, they supported and encouraged her more than the ordinary people.

One of the most intriguing aspects is her ordinariness. She was a middle-class woman from a prosperous town. The experiences of people like this rarely survive from the Middle Ages, and it is the unashamed honesty and earthiness of Margery's book that has captivated readers since the discovery of the only surviving manuscript of her work in 1934. Had it not been for this chance discovery, we would have little sense of this woman and her astonishing life, nor the insights into the domestic life of the time that she reveals. There is a bench in her name on the Saturday Market Place, which was commissioned by the Civic Society.

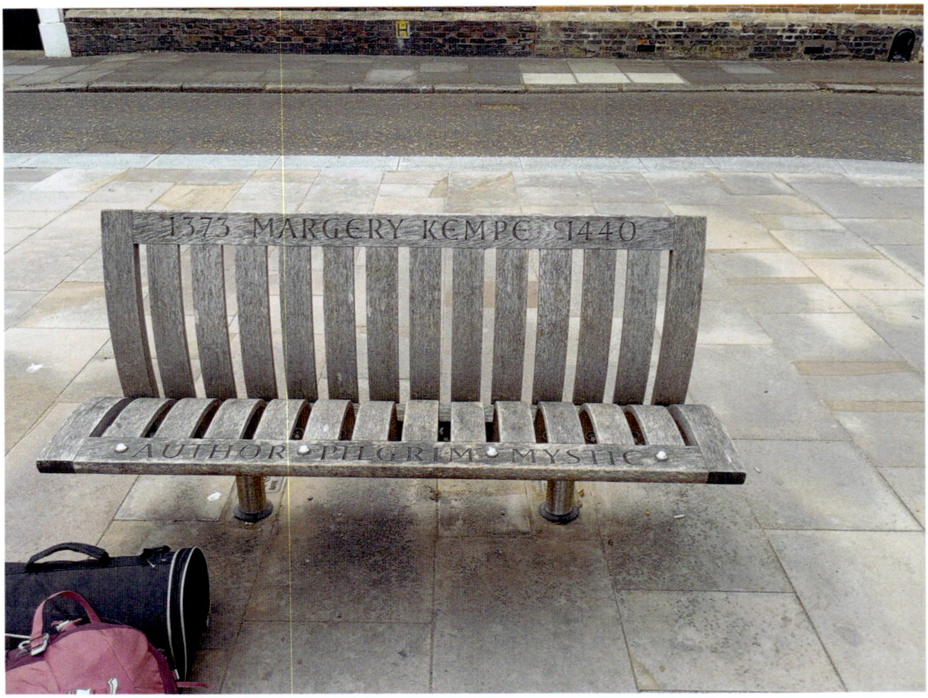

Saturday Market Place bench commemorating Margery Kempe.

Unusual Buildings and Structures

Stock Fish Rack

This artwork stands on South Quay by Marriott's Warehouse. It was commissioned by West Norfolk Council and created by the British Artist Blacksmith Association in an epic collaboration. The sculpture came into being during the town's first Hanse Festival in summer 2009 and as part of the celebrations, 150 blacksmiths congregated on the quay and created the fish racks under the direction of Nigel Barnett (born 1964) of Fransham Forge, Great Fransham, Norfolk. This must have been an amazing sight to see and hear. The tall double-frame rack has four racks on each side from which hang an array of seventy-six marine objects, mostly fish, but including oysters, a spiky mine, seaweed and a mermaid's bra, under the keen eye of a gull. It represents the history of 'stock fish', the name given to dried cod that used to constitute a flourishing trade on the quay alongside the Great Ouse River in King's Lynn. The fish came from the Lofoten Islands, north of Bergen, where it was dried on racks, a centuries old process that produced a top grade product with high concentrations of protein. As far back as 1300 it was carried to Lynn and Boston in Hanseatic ships from where it was distributed inland, mainly by river.

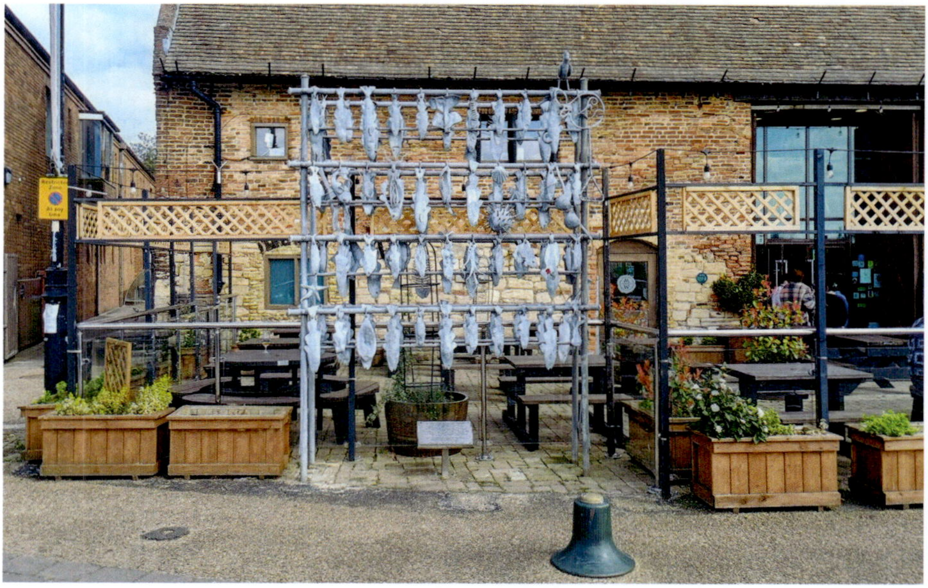

Stock Fish Rack sculpture, a real blacksmithing tour de force.

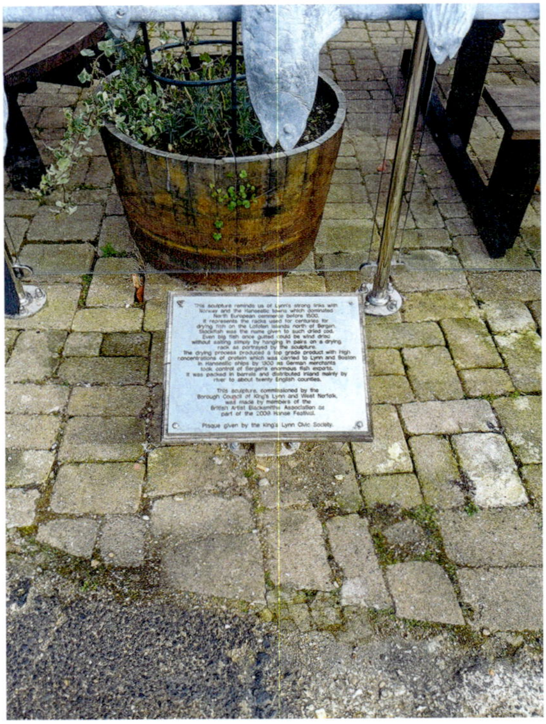

Plaque commemorating a fantastic team effort.

Marriott's Warehouse

Marriott's Warehouse is thought to have been built in its present form around 1580. It is now run by a trust, a charitable organisation which manages the building on behalf of the Borough Council of King's Lynn and West Norfolk. It holds a lease from the borough council for the building and provides a licence to Marriott's Warehouse Restaurant, which is a business in its own right. The licence provides the restaurant with the ground and first floors, together with the outside area. The restaurant opened on 14 April 2013. However, the licence agreement allows for permanent access by the trust for members of the public to the meeting room and model exhibitions in other parts of the building. The exhibitions of models feature iconic local buildings and a townscape by local carpenter Fred Hall. The trust's meeting room is also used by various community groups and regularly has presentations on topics of local interest, under the guise of 'Trust Talks'. Incorporating stone from the demolished friaries of Lynn, the brick warehouse was originally constructed by the Clayborne family to store their corn, salt and wine. It is Grade II* listed and takes its name from the Marriott brothers who owned or leased several granaries on the South Quay in the nineteenth century. As maritime trade patterns changed, the warehouse fell into reduced use and eventual disrepair. Restoration was undertaken in the late 1990s.

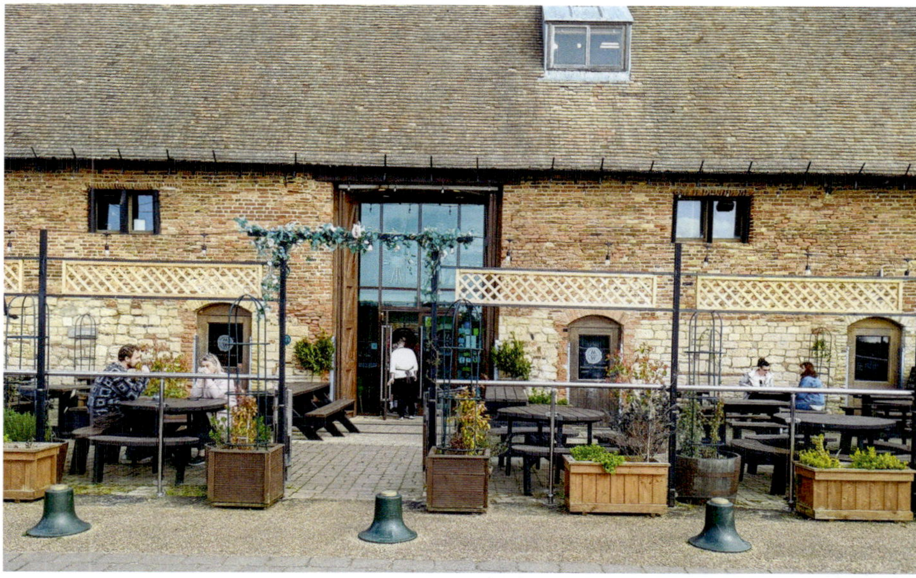

Marriott's Warehouse – not just a restaurant.

Greenland Fishery

'Atkin's Mansion' was built in 1605 by wealthy merchant John Atkin, who was twice mayor of the borough. The house was built in a prominent position on what was then the main route into King's Lynn from the south. It remained in the Atkins family until his grandson, Thomas Atkin 'of London', sold it. It was certainly a grand house, possibly the last great timber-framed house to be built in Lynn, with enormous brick chimney stacks. The first-floor hall ran the length of the building and was lit by oriel windows. The house was subsequently divided into two, the southern portion becoming a public house called 'The Fisherman's Arms' or 'The Waterman's Arms'. By 1796 it had been renamed the 'The Greenland Fishery Inn' to mark the importance of the whaling industry to the town during those years (1770s–1820s) when a small fleet was sent out to Greenland and the Davis Straits to fish for whales and seals. By 1900 the house was in poor condition, deemed unfit for habitation, and in 1911 the owners were ordered to repair it or demolish it. They offered it to the borough council for £50 but the offer was declined, probably because the repair bill was estimated at £300. It was rescued in 1912 by G. M. Beloe, a local solicitor and historian, who bought the whole complex, street range (including a baker's shop), small former pub called 'The Cottage' and further land at the back. Beloe restored the whole building and set up the Greenland Fishery Museum on the first and second floors. It was opened on 6 June 1912 by the Earl of Oxford and housed an extensive collection of items purchased by him and his father. Beloe recognised the value of domestic and agricultural implements and tools that were going out of use. His collection included the relics of Eugene Aram, paintings by local artists, pilgrim badges and whalebones.

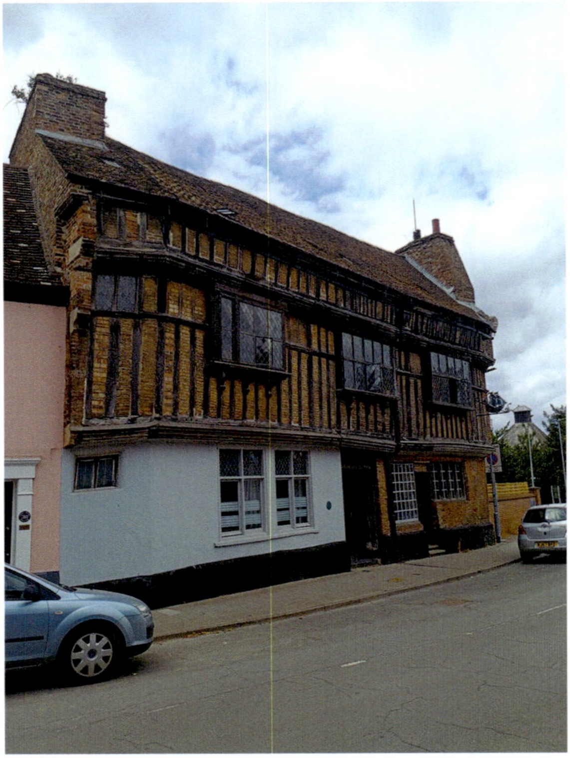

Greenland Fishery – warehouse, pub, bakers, museum and now a music centre.

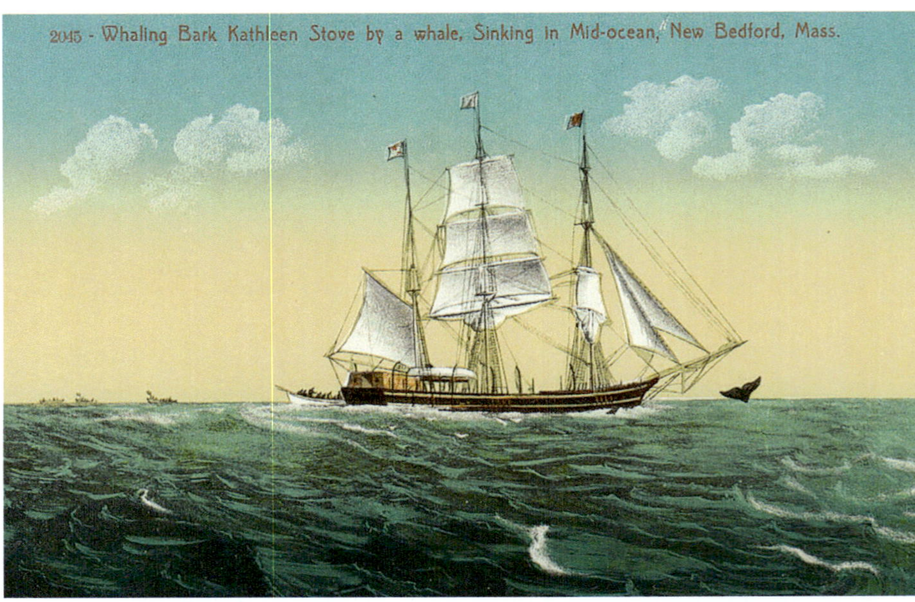

Whaling bark *Kathleen*, stove by a whale, sinking in mid-ocean, New Bedford, Mass, 1900–1910. (Library of Congress)

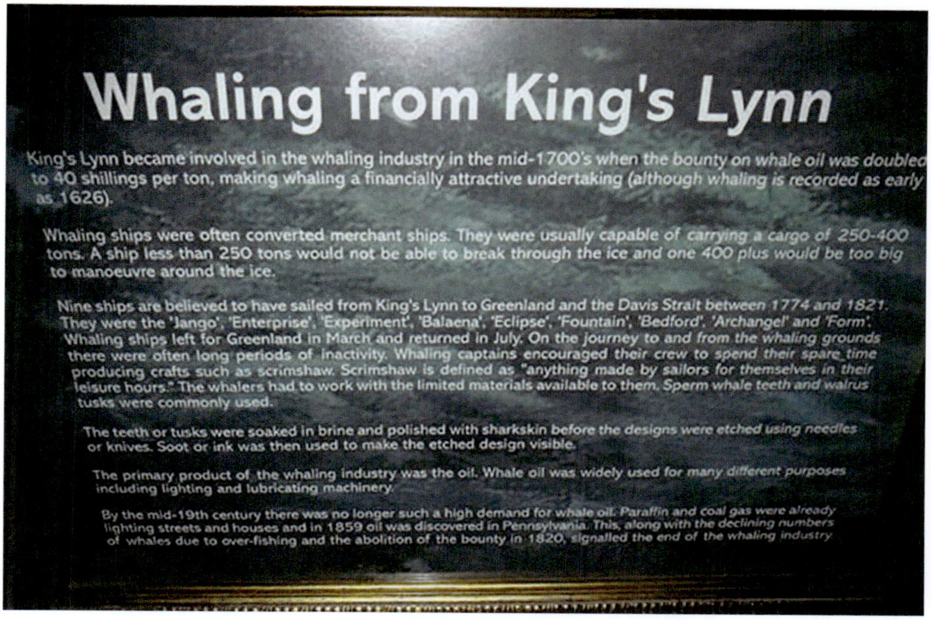

'Whaling from King's Lynn' information board in the 'Whalebone' Downham Market. (Courtesy of J. D. Wetherspoon)

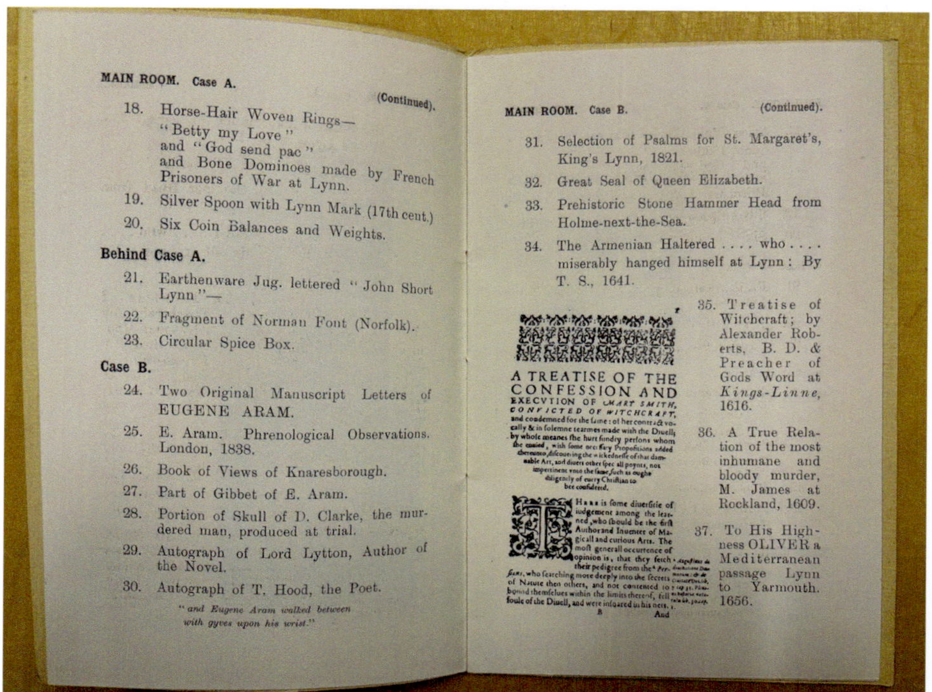

MAIN ROOM. Case A. (Continued).

18. Horse-Hair Woven Rings— "Betty my Love" and "God send pac" and Bone Dominoes made by French Prisoners of War at Lynn.
19. Silver Spoon with Lynn Mark (17th cent.)
20. Six Coin Balances and Weights.

Behind Case A.

21. Earthenware Jug. lettered "John Short Lynn"—
22. Fragment of Norman Font (Norfolk).
23. Circular Spice Box.

Case B.

24. Two Original Manuscript Letters of EUGENE ARAM.
25. E. Aram. Phrenological Observations. London, 1838.
26. Book of Views of Knaresborough.
27. Part of Gibbet of E. Aram.
28. Portion of Skull of D. Clarke, the murdered man, produced at trial.
29. Autograph of Lord Lytton, Author of the Novel.
30. Autograph of T. Hood, the Poet.

"and Eugene Aram walked between with gyves upon his wrist."

MAIN ROOM. Case B. (Continued).

31. Selection of Psalms for St. Margaret's, King's Lynn, 1821.
32. Great Seal of Queen Elizabeth.
33. Prehistoric Stone Hammer Head from Holme-next-the-Sea.
34. The Armenian Haltered .... who .... miserably hanged himself at Lynn: By T. S., 1641.
35. Treatise of Witchcraft; by Alexander Roberts, B. D. & Preacher of Gods Word at *Kings-Linne*, 1616.
36. A True Relation of the most inhumane and bloody murder, M. James at Rockland, 1609.
37. To His Highness OLIVER a Mediterranean passage Lynn to Yarmouth. 1656.

A TREATISE OF THE CONFESSION AND EXECVTION OF MARY SMITH, CONVICTED OF WITCHCRAFT, and condemned for the same: of her contract vocally & in solemne tearmes made with the Diuell, by whose meanes she hurt sundry persons whom she enuied, with some necessary Propositions added thereunto, discouering the wickednesse of that damnable Art, and diuers other speciall poynts, not impertinent vnto the same, such as ought diligently of euery Christian to bee considered.

THere is some diuersitie of iudgement among the learned, who should be the first Author and Inuenter of Magicall and curious Arts. The most generall occurrence of opinion is, that they fetch their pedigree from the Persians, who searching more deeply into the secrets of Nature then others, and not contented to bound themselues within the limits thereof, fell into the Diuell, and were insnared in his nets.

B And

An extract from the Greenland Fishery Museum guide from 1926. (Courtesy of Norfolk Museums Service, Lynn Museum, King's Lynn)

On 16 August 1759, Eugene Aram (1704–59), a former King's Lynn Grammar School teacher, was hanged for the murder of his former friend some fourteen years earlier. Aram was born in Ramsgill, Yorkshire, in 1704, and although he came from a very poor background, the boy initially obtained access to books via different employers. Over time, he managed to teach himself Latin, Greek, Hebrew, Chaldee, Arabic, and several Celtic languages. In later life he recognised truths that were not admitted by scholars for another hundred or so years, namely that Latin was not derived from Greek, and that the Celtic languages were related to other European languages. While he was still young, Aram's girlfriend became pregnant and he married her. He eventually settled as a schoolmaster at Netherdale. In 1734 he moved to Knaresborough, where he remained as schoolmaster until 1744. In that year, Aram became embroiled in a local scandal that eventually caused him to leave his wife and seven children in Knaresborough and move to London. A close friend of Aram's, a shoemaker called Daniel Clark, was thought to have come into a considerable amount of money from his wife. On the basis of this rumour, Clark purchased a variety of valuable goods on credit. Unfortunately, Clark suddenly disappeared with the goods, and at the same time, Aram started to settle many of his own debts. As one of his closest friends, Aram had been questioned about the activities of the swindling shoemaker, but could shed no light on Clark's current whereabouts. The discovery of some of the missing goods in Aram's garden may have been a little compromising, but Aram said that Clark himself had left them there. With no evidence to suggest otherwise, the official enquiries ended there. For several years Aram travelled through parts of England, teaching in a number of schools. In February 1758, King's Lynn Grammar School welcomed Aram as its new schoolmaster. The building was modest. The school was housed in a room above the Charnel Chapel on the Saturday Market Place adjacent to the St Margaret's Church. However, the new teacher came with very impressive qualifications, and by this time, he was he doubtless hoping that any hint of scandal had long been left behind.

In February 1758 a local workman in Knaresborough was digging for stone and discovered a whole skeleton. The local police remembered the strange disappearance of Daniel Clark and went to talk to Aram's estranged wife. She had long since felt that her husband had something to do with Clark's disappearance. She also gave the name of Richard Houseman as a possible accomplice. Mrs Aram now revealed that she found her husband burning clothes in the garden on the day after Clark's disappearance. When questioned by the police, Houseman indicated he knew the skeleton was not Daniel Clark because he knew where Clark was in fact buried, in St Robert's Cave, a well-known spot near Knaresborough. Houseman also said that Aram had killed the shoemaker. A horse trader recognised Aram in Lynn and reported his location back to Yorkshire. Two constables, John Barker and Francis Moore, were dispatched to the Norfolk town. When approached by the constables Aram panicked and denied that he had ever known Clark. He was arrested on the spot on 21 August 1758. Prior to his trial on his journey north he had protested his innocence. He now admitted that he really had known Daniel Clark, but he said that had no connection with the shoemaker's fraudulent activity and he had no idea what had happened to Clark. His three-day trial began on 3 August 1759 at York County Court. Aram chose to defend himself through a prepared statement. He did not try to overthrow Houseman's evidence, but argued a man of his education and academic standing would not be involved in murder. He lacked motive, being more interested in study than in wealth, and he disputed that Clark was even dead. The argument about the uncertainty of the identity of the skeleton may seem valid and, of course, a modern jury would require more in the way of forensic evidence. However, this jury were not convinced by the academic, and Aram was found guilty and condemned. The jury came to their conclusion without even having to leave the courtroom. While in his cell awaiting death Aram confessed to the murder and threw light on his motive. He said he had good reason to suspect an affair between Clark and his wife. It was a crime of passion that he deeply regretted. On the day before his execution, he had unsuccessfully tried to kill himself by opening his veins with a razor. Eugene Aram was hanged in York at Tyburn Prison on 16 August 1759. Aram's body was then gibbeted

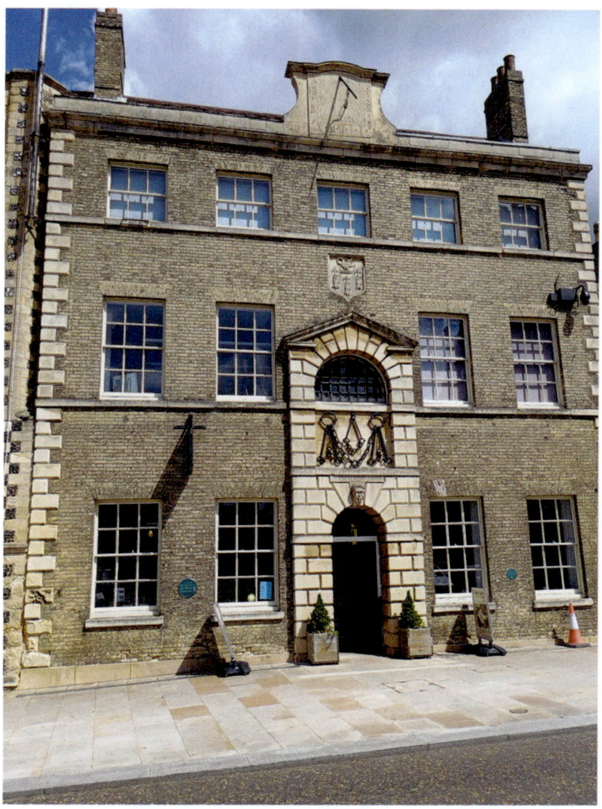

Stories of Lynn where the skull of Eugene Aram is on display in the Old Gaol section.

(hung in chains) in Knaresborough Forest. His skull was acquired in the 1830s by a man called Hutchinson, a local doctor. It passed through several hands before eventually being returned to King's Lynn in 1993, when it was gifted to the town by the Royal College of Surgeons. It now sits in the Old Gaol section of the 'Stories of Lynn' exhibition near the site where Aram briefly taught. The murderer is celebrated by Thomas Hood in his ballad 'The Dream of Eugene Aram', and by Edward Bulwer-Lytton in his 1832 novel *Eugene Aram*.

Downstairs housed a baker's shop run by a Mr Lewis, baking his wares in the basement kitchen. Visitors had to enter through the shop and Mrs Lewis, who was the museum's caretaker, would encourage the trying and purchase of her husband's ships biscuits. Following Beloe's death in 1932, his widow sold the building and contents to the Norfolk Archaeological Trust and borough council jointly. The museum continued until it was damaged by a bomb in 1941. After the wartime damage, some of the collection was passed to the Lynn Museum. Some of the notable items are the pilgrim badges. These small, metal badges date from the medieval period and could be purchased by pilgrims at the religious shrines they visited. The majority of this collection is on permanent display at

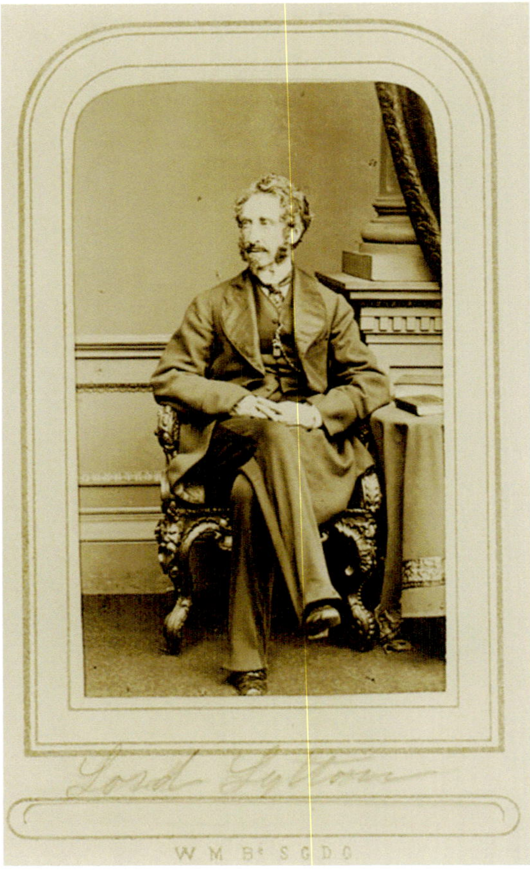

Edward Bulwer-Lytton (1803–73). His most famous quotation is 'The pen is mightier than the sword' from his play *Richelieu*. Published between 1860 and 1869. (Library of Congress)

Lynn Museum. Some of the Aram material also came across to that institution. I am indebted to Dayna Woolbright, Newman Curator, Lynn Museum, for this information. It was left empty but scheduled as an ancient monument in 1945. After the war it was restored and converted into a house and an office.

Miss M. Keith and Miss Diana Bullock were the first tenants and expert gardeners, and they created a wonderful town garden behind the house. Both ladies were involved in the Preservation Trust and their home became the trust's first registered office. Miss Bullock died in 1994. In 1997, the Norfolk Archaeological Trust transferred the building to the trust for a nominal payment and restoration commenced. The works included a careful overhaul of one of the house's best kept secrets: a series of the fine Jacobean wall paintings. In 2023 The Lynn Preservation Trust puts Greenland Fishery on the market on a 999-year lease for £400,000. At the time, the trust said that the building was not suitable for short-term leases. The property was described as having two self-contained units, a large two-bedroom residence at No. 29 Bridge Street and commercial office premises at No. 28 Bridge Street. They were set over three floors and there were cellars under most of the property. The historic building was eventually bought by musician Stevie Wishart, who has been making efforts to bring the building back to life.

Stevie Wishart is a composer, improviser and performer on the hurdy-gurdy and violin. Mainly involved in contemporary music, she has also had a career in early music. The Grade II listed building near Boal Quay is set to become an 'inspirational place' for musicians and composers in the borough to gather. Currently, works are taking place by Stevie and her team to make 'Greenland Fishery' a vibrant place to be once again.

The Athenaeum

The Gurney family of Quaker bankers founded the Athenaeum in King's Lynn in 1854. This community centre contained, amongst other things, a public library and museum, which allowed both working-class and more affluent readers access to reading material and knowledge. The purpose of the King's Lynn Athenaeum was detailed in the *Lynn Advertiser*, which said it was planned to 'Unite under one roof the several literary, scientific, and artistic societies in the town', and it accommodated the library, museum, an institute (or newsroom) and the Conversazione, a society that discussed literature and the arts. It was not just societies that made use of the Athenaeum though. Within the building, a central hall was constructed with the intention of hosting lectures, concerts and exhibitions for the public to attend. The following decades saw numerous music hall acts grace the stage, along with classical concerts that featured artists and opera singers from Italy, Vienna and Russia, and special guest lecturers frequently added the Athenaeum to their tour. One such lecturer, who gave a talk in 1884 entitled 'Personal Impressions of America' was Oscar Wilde. Wilde's talk was one of the first to occur after parts of the Athenaeum had been taken over as a post office and telegraph station. Despite the dazzling acts and famous faces

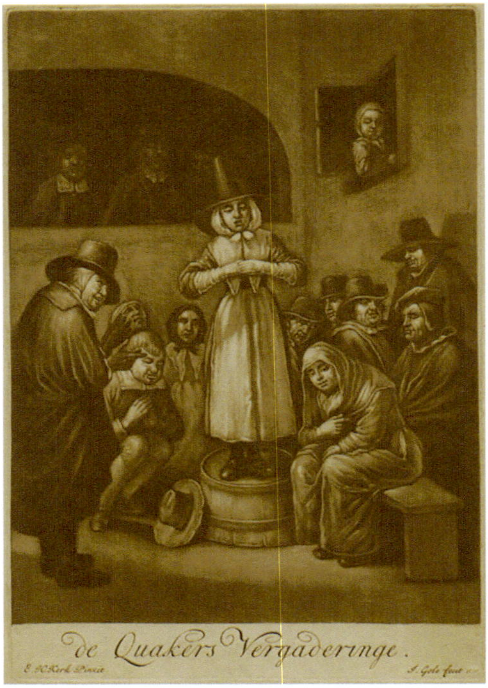

'The Quakers Meeting' print made by Jacob Gole (1660–1737). (Yale Center for British Art)

appearing on stage, it was not as big of a commercial success as everyone had hoped when the building first opened. This led to parts of it being sold to the post office, although events and concerts still went ahead, and the societies were still accommodated for.

It was not until 1936 that the Athenaeum was no longer an institution for the arts, and instead was sold fully to become the town's Telephone Exchange and Post Office. Renovations on the building modified it and, bizarrely enough, elm and beech panelling used in the interior offices had come from the bed of the River Thames during the demolition of Waterloo Bridge in 1934; materials that were not needed for the new bridge were recycled across the country. Indeed, there was even a plaque within the post office to commemorate this odd anecdote:

> The joinery in this public office is made of silver beech and elm taken from the original piles of Waterloo Bridge London where it was immersed in the riverbed for about 120 years. It was recovered from the river in 1936.

In 2007 the Athenaeum closed for good when the post office relocated to WHSmith. However, there may be a new beginning for this old institution, as planning permission has been applied for to convert it into a pub with flats above it. If work goes ahead, thirty flats will be built across the first, second and third floors, with a pub, wine bar, other drinking premises and a hot food takeaway being set up in the ground floor.

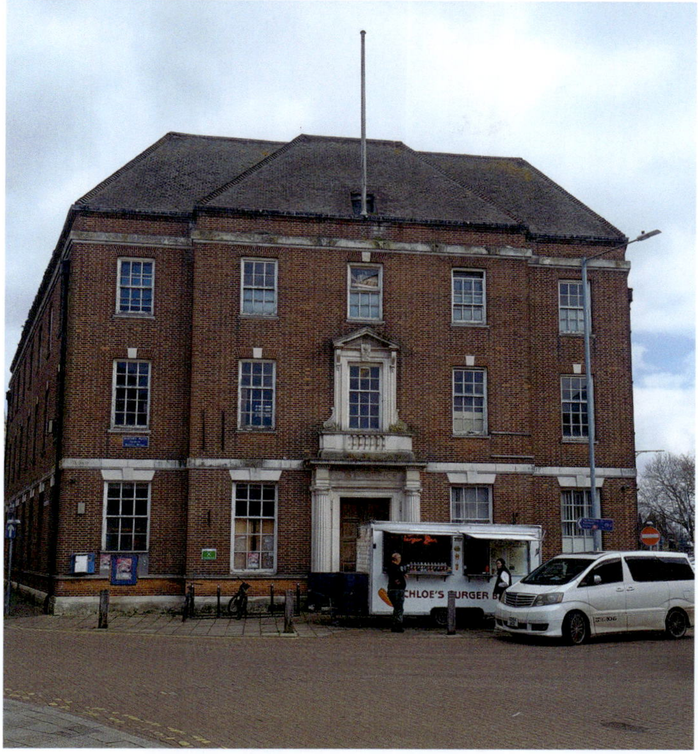

The former Athenaeum. Renovation is on its way.

Whitefriars Gate

Whitefriars Gate in King's Lynn is the sole remaining structure of the former Carmelite Friary. The gate, a single brick arch with stone dressings, is preserved on the side of a modern footpath. The Friary buildings were located within the town's defensive walls, and the gate was part of the precinct wall. The members of the Order of the Friars of Our Lady of Mount Carmel, or the Carmelites, were also known as White Friars, because of the white mantles and cowls they wore over their habits. They were actually cream. They were not monks, such as the Benedictines or Cistercians. Monks often settled in more remote areas, but the friars lived and worked in towns, where they concentrated on preaching and hearing confessions. They were very learned and, for many, part of their training was to study at Oxford or Cambridge. They were poor at first; their income came from begging for alms in towns and from legacies and not from vast agricultural estates such as the monks possessed. They became well liked and had frequent skirmishes with the ordinary clergy, whose congregations they were taking. The Carmelites seem to have begun as a group of hermits on Mount Carmel in Palestine in the twelfth century. As they migrated, they were living by a formal Rule by about 1210 and, when they first came to Britain in the 1240s, they were still seeking what were then remote areas to settle in, such as Alnwick in Northumberland, Aylesford in Kent and Burnham Norton in Norfolk.

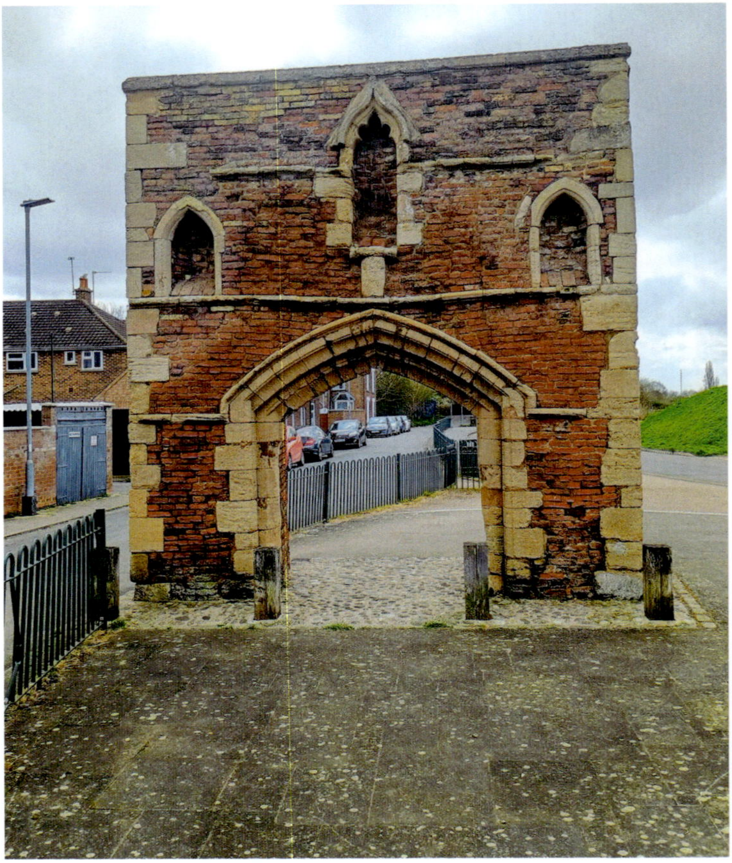

Whitefriars Gate. Like a single tooth in an old man's mouth – a beautiful one though.

They were reformed on the Dominican model by their English General of the Order, St Simon Stock, in the 1260s and gave up their hermit life and began to work in towns. The friars soon became rich and popular. One method of fundraising that they employed was to set up a fraternity whereby, for a sum, the wealthy could take on some aspects of the Carmelites' Rule, and would ultimately be interred in their church.

The house of the White Friars or Carmelites stood on the south side of the town, close to the River Lynn. The earliest record mention of it occurs in 1261 in a document relative to the obstruction of a lane. In the fourteenth century there is mention of two stretches of cloister, an infirmary, refectory and residence with a garden. A church and cemetery were on the northern part of the site. The friary was dissolved in 1538. The northern gateway is the only significant survival from the buildings. The gateway is dated fifteenth century, built of brick and ashlar dressing, and the north side has two storeys in elevation but not the south. The gateway is a Grade II listed building. The name lives on at Whitefriars Church of England Primary Academy in Whitefriars Road, Carmelite Terrace and Whitefriars Terrace.

Austin Friars Gate

In Austin Street are the blocked-up remains of an arched gateway. This is the only surviving evidence of the Augustinian Priory, which was founded in 1295 and dissolved in 1538. The Augustinian religious organisation, who were also named Austin Friars, were originally hermits. They were clothed in black and observed the rule of St Augustine.

Augustine of Hippo was perhaps the greatest Christian philosopher of antiquity and certainly the one who exerted the deepest and most lasting influence. He is a saint of the Catholic Church, and his authority in theological matters was universally accepted in the Latin Middle Ages and remained, in the Western Christian tradition, virtually uncontested until the nineteenth century. He is the patron saint of brewers because of his conversion from a former life of loose living, which included parties, entertainment and worldly ambitions. His complete turnaround and conversion have been an inspiration to many who struggle with a particular vice or habit they long to break. The Order of Saint Augustine was founded in 1244 by bringing together several groups in the Tuscany region. They are also known as Augustinians, Austin Friars, or Friars Hermits and were historically known as the Order of Hermits of Saint Augustine. This order of Mendicants first appeared in England about the year 1250. The Austin Friars settled at Lynn early in the reign of Edward I, on the north side of the town. They were well established by 1295. The Augustinian Friary, also

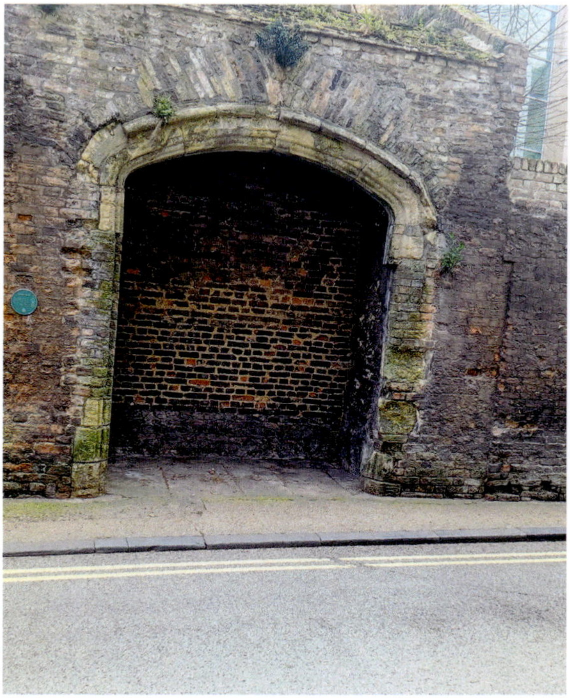

Remains of Austin Friars Gate, now a medieval shelter against the rain.

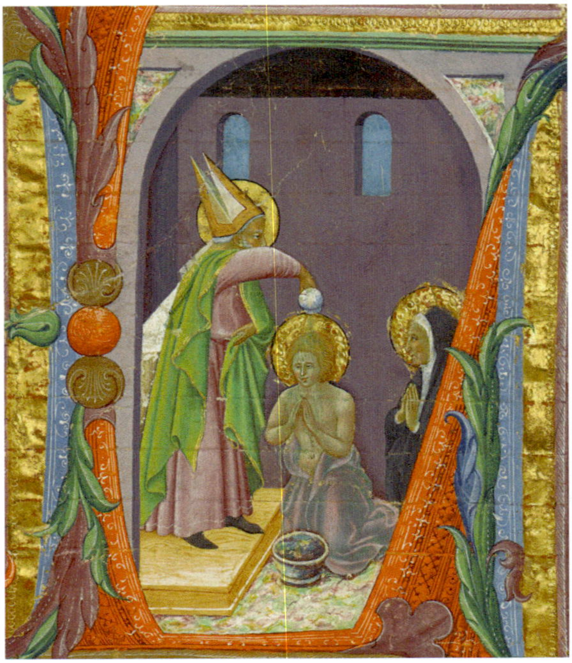

Initial L: The Baptism of Saint Augustine, Master of the Osservanza, illuminator (Italian, active second quarter of the fifteenth century), c. 1430. (Getty Search Gateway)

called Austin Friars, was the largest of the friaries in King's Lynn and the most prestigious. It was founded in 1293 on land given to them by Margaret de Southmere. In 1383 King Richard III granted a licence to the friary to build an aqueduct to bring them a supply of fresh water from Gaywood. The luxury of fresh water was being granted to a friary, whilst the general populace would have had to use salt water and drink small, fresh, cloudy ale.

Over the next few years (1406–13) the Augustinians added to the site, which was an indicator of their wealth and influence. The order was renowned for its 'exceedingly profitable altar' also called the *Scala Coeli* (stairway to heaven). Henry V and VI were well-known visitors to the friary, together with Henry VII and his queen, Elizabeth of York. Margaret Beaufort and Arthur, Prince of Wales, also stayed here.

In the present day, as of 2024, there are four Augustinian communities around the United Kingdom: St Mary's, Harbourne; Clare Priory, in Suffolk; St Augustine's Church, Hammersmith; and St Monica's Church, Hoxton. There are around twenty Augustinian friars in total serving in the United Kingdom, who involved in a variety of ministries, including prison and university chaplaincy. Clare Priory serves as a parish and retreat centre and also houses a shrine dedicated to Our Lady, Mother of Good Counsel. There is also a community of Augustinian canonesses at Boarbank Hall in Cumbria.

In King's Lynn, their name lives on in Austin Street and Austin Fields Industrial Estate, a popular commercial trading estate located near the town centre.

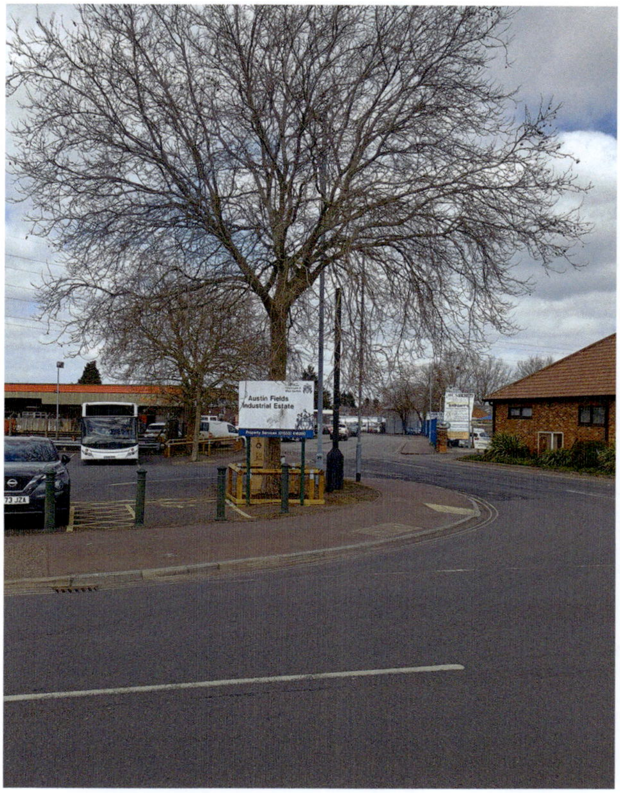

Austin Fields Industrial Estate – another legacy of the friars.

Greyfriars Tower

Of the sixty Franciscan friaries that existed in England prior to the suppression in 1538, significant remains of only sixteen exist. Greyfriars Tower is one of only three remaining in the country, and is the most attractive and complete. The tower is a key landmark in King's Lynn and it owes its survival to the fact it proved a useful seamark for traders and sailors navigating the difficult waters of The Wash. With Grade I listed/Scheduled Ancient Monument status, the tower is located in the attractive Tower Gardens on land formerly within the boundary of the friary. The gardens were laid out in 1911 to mark the coronation of King George V. They also contain the former Public Library, completed in 1905, and the King's Lynn War Memorial, designed in 1921.The Tower Gardens have been remodelled utilising hard landscaping to indicate the location and extent of the nave, north aisle, chancel, cloister walks and chapter house enhancing interpretation and awareness of the complex. The tower featured as a finalist on the BBC programme *Restoration* in 2003 to bid for funding to restore and maintain it. Although the bid was not successful, monies were forthcoming from English Heritage and the Heritage Lottery Fund and the tower is now safely refurbished. Restoration and enhancement of the leaning tower and gardens was completed in 2006.

The Grey Friars, or Franciscans, are followers of St Francis of Assisi, patron saint of animals, merchants and ecology, born at Assisi in Umbria in 1181 or 1182 (the exact year is uncertain) and died there on 3 October 1226. They founded many religious houses across Europe and earned their name from the grey habits that were worn as a symbol of their vow of poverty. They came to England in 1224, around a year before the death of St Francis of Assisi, their founder. In 1235 a priory of Franciscan monks was established in King's Lynn. The priory was suppressed in 1538 by Henry VIII during his Dissolution of the Monasteries, along with the town's three other friaries, run by the Augustinians, the Dominicans and the Carmelites. Unlike monastic orders such as the Cistercians, who established their abbeys far from centres of population, the Grey Friars lived among the people, preaching and teaching to the local population. They took vows of poverty and relied on donations from local people to survive. Greyfriars was a medium-sized friary, supporting thirty-eight friars in 1325. In the early years of the fourteenth century, the friars designed a system of conduits to bring fresh water from a spring at North Runcton, over a mile away. The friary grounds were surrounded by a high stone wall, entered through an imposing gatehouse.

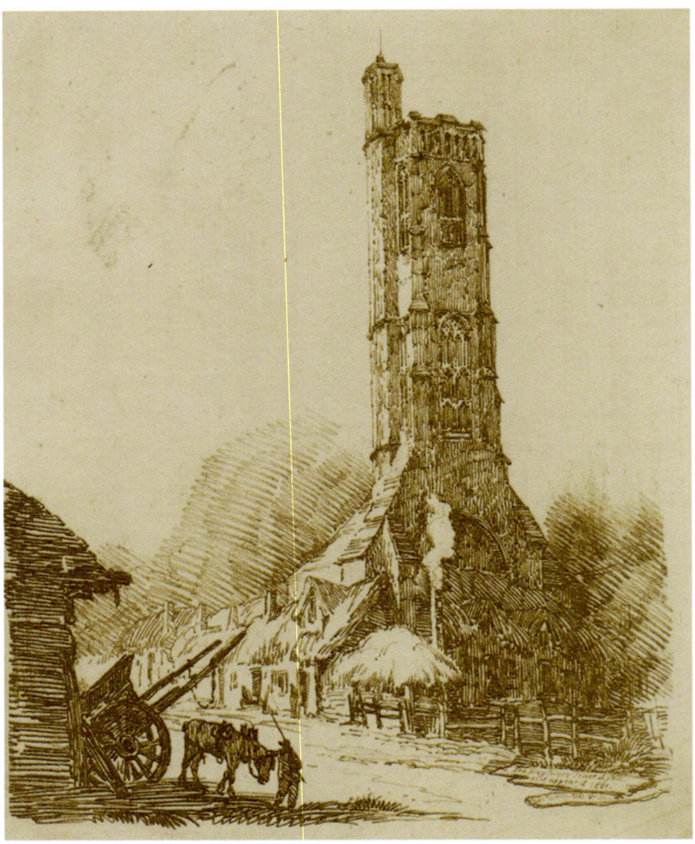

Greyfriars Tower, King's Lynn, as it appeared in 1801, by Robert Dixon (1780–1815). (Yale Center for British Art)

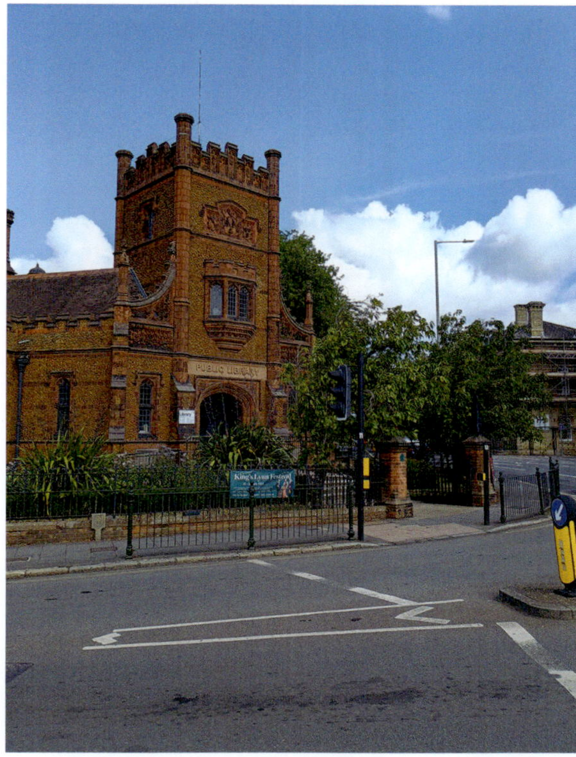

The former central library. It was opened by Andrew Carnegie in 1905. It cost £5,000 to build and is one of 660 Carnegie libraries in the UK and Ireland.

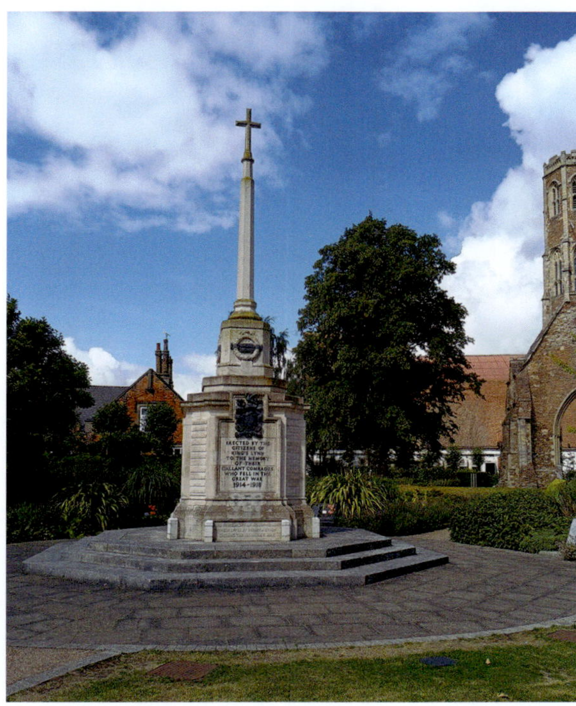

King's Lynn War Memorial. The war memorial was first dedicated and unveiled on 26 January 1921 by HRH Princess Mary.

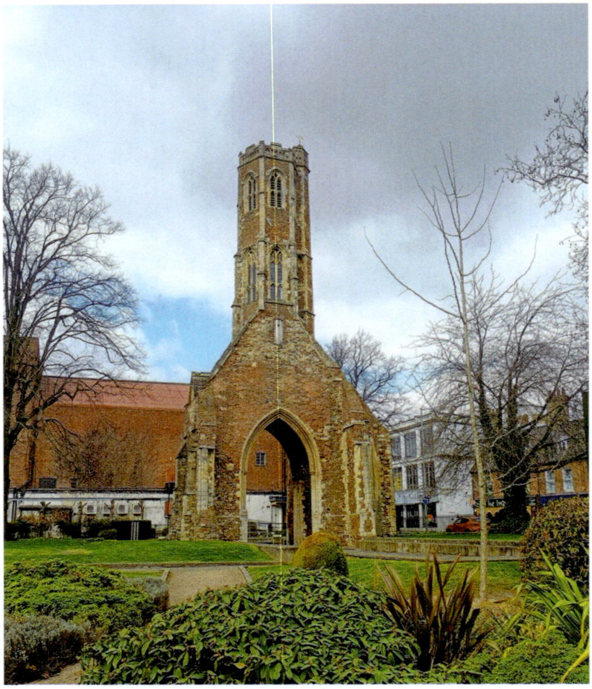

The restored Greyfriars Tower today set in beautiful gardens.

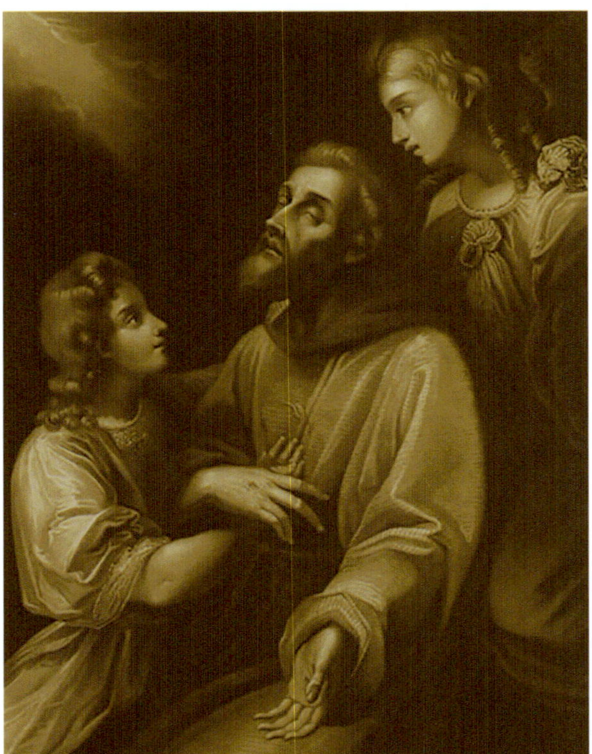

St Francis of Assisi, an Italian mystic, poet and Catholic friar. *The Ecstasy of St Francis*, 1809, print made by William Say (1768–1834). (Yale Center of British Art)

The Greyfriars still exist today and have diverse roles and responsibilities within their ministry. They may serve as parish priests, chaplains, educators in schools, hospital administrators, or aid the poor. However, their range of duties extends beyond these examples. The order is founded on religious profession, through which the friars dedicate themselves to living a life of perfect charity as guided by the Gospel. This commitment goes beyond ordinary means of sanctification and is expressed through the public vows of poverty, chastity and obedience. By these vows, the friars are consecrated to God through the ministry of the Church, and by the observance of fraternity, the rule, and constitutions. Friars are definitively incorporated into the order by their profession of these solemn vows.

Clifton House

Clifton House is thought by many to the be finest surviving merchant house in King's Lynn. Built in a prime position, fronting onto Queen Street and backing onto the river, the site has been occupied since the twelfth century. The present house gains its name from William Clifton and his heir, who owned it for much of the nineteenth century, but owes it grandeur to the Taylor family, who remodelled it at the turn of the eighteen century. The current house occupies the site of two or three medieval properties, features of which remain incorporated in the structure. The first clue to the wealth and importance of these early owners is revealed below the house, where there is a fine brick-vaulted undercroft dating from the mid-fourteenth century. This would have been used by the merchant owners as a storage area for their goods. Within one wall of the undercroft the remains of a twelfth-century window, the clue to an earlier building, can be seen. Equally significant, a medieval tiled floor was found under what is now the kitchen, but would formerly have been a parlour. The tiles, dating from the late thirteenth century, are of the type known as 'Westminster tiles' and are extremely rare, particularly in a domestic building. The then owners were undoubtedly wealthy and important people. During Tudor times the five-storey tower was constructed, probably by a Lynn merchant by the name of George Walden, who owned the property in the 1570s. Entry was from the riverside yard rather than the house, but it was more than just a watchtower and office. The tower was a status symbol, used to entertain guests and associates, its rich decorations and fine views intended to impress. The last significant change to the site can be credited to the Taylor family. Simon Taylor, a loyal royalist during the reign of Charles II, was both MP for Lynn and knighted by the king in 1684. He set about remodelling the family home, which he had owned since the early 1660s. It was his son and heir, Samuel Taylor, who completed the project. It is believed that they employed architect Henry Bell to undertake the work. The scheme included remodelling the street fronts in a grand style, with sash windows and a magnificent doorcase. The doorcase, with unusual twisted barley sugar columns made from mahogany and known as Solomonic columns, leads to the terrace adjacent to the house and frames the entrance to the tower, also designed by Bell. The redesign of the interior included the insertion of a magnificent central staircase.

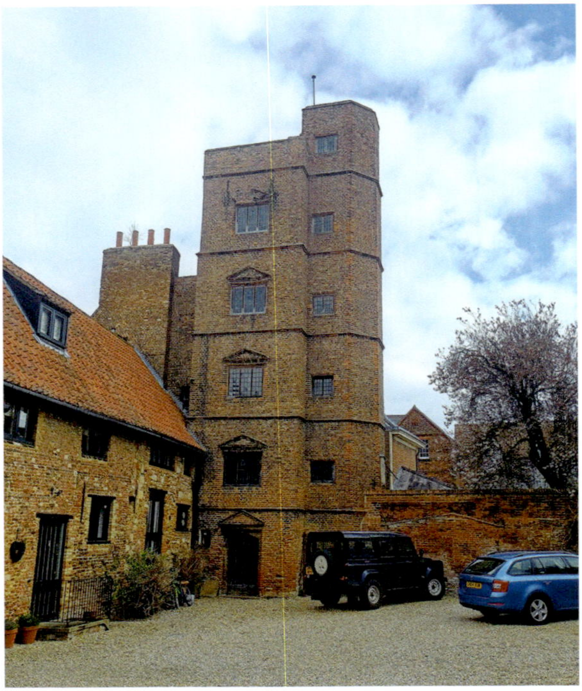

The Tower, Clifton House. A five-storey Elizabethan watchtower that was built in the late sixteenth century.

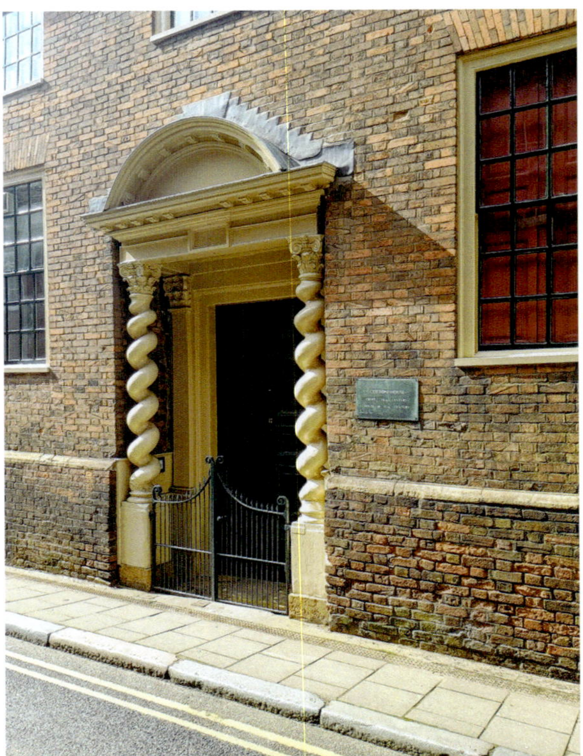

Barley twist pillars on the front entrance to Clifton House, made from mahogany, and known as Solomonic columns. A rare baroque motif in England.

Sadly, the nineteenth and twentieth centuries saw a slow decline of the house. Some respite was afforded in the 1960s and 1970s when the property was owned by King's Lynn Borough Council and the long-lost medieval floor tiles were discovered and saved. The house was sold into private hands in 1982. With the death of the owner, the house came onto the market in 1996. The King's Lynn Preservation Trust had long been concerned about the steady deterioration of this magnificent house and made the decision to purchase it. Urgent repairs were needed to make it weather and sound proof. Whilst seeking grant funding the trust pressed on with repairing the roof, treating the timber and replacing fallen ceilings. Brickwork in both house and tower needed repairs, along with window frames. The arrival of a grant from English Heritage, which covered a portion of the costs, was most welcome. Once the exterior and urgent works were completed, the trust decided to sell the house. They were especially keen to see it go to an owner who would complete the restoration and use it as a family home. In 2005 the house was sold to Dr Simon Thurley, then CEO of English Heritage, and his wife Dr Anna Keay, an architectural historian. They proved to be the perfect custodians of the house, turning it into their much-loved family home. They have undertaken a painstaking restoration of the interiors of the house and tower, revealing further layers of history in the process. They have been generous in sharing their findings with others. The house is open to view on Heritage Open Day, during the annual King's Lynn Festival and at other times by arrangement with the owners.

Old Savings Bank

The former Lynn Savings Bank building was completed in 1858 and the imposing design was meant to give a feeling of reassurance after some traumatic decades for banks. It was designed by Alfred Maberley, a London-born architect who went into partnership with the King's Lynn Cruso's, who were surveyors. By 1855, the partnership had been dissolved and Maberley was now part of Medland and Maberley of Gloucester and this new partnership designed the Savings Bank. The bank had been trading since October 1817 from their previous premises at No. 118 High Street in the town and was later absorbed into the Trustee Savings Bank. The town's pelican symbol, which is on the King's Lynn coat of arms, is on the central corbel of the building, all designed to give it that feeling of security. The building is of huge importance as the first savings bank to continue the external Tudor Gothic design into the interior rather than having a standard inside layout. Internally there is a huge stone fireplace. The exterior style of design in itself was rare in the town at the time. The King's Lynn YMCA purchased the old Savings Bank in 1891 and added a gymnasium and lecture hall. On 4 March 1891 the building was formally opened as the new home of the YMCA by J. J. Colman, MP for Norwich and President of Norwich YMCA.

For thirty years the building was a clubhouse for the Lynn branch of the Royal Antediluvian Order of Buffaloes until 2015. They are now believed to be based at Hamburg Way, King's Lynn. The RAOB is a philanthropic fraternal organisation that provides aid to its members, their families, and other charitable organizations. The order has a history dating back to 1822 and is known to its members as the 'Buffs'. The premises have now been converted into four apartments.

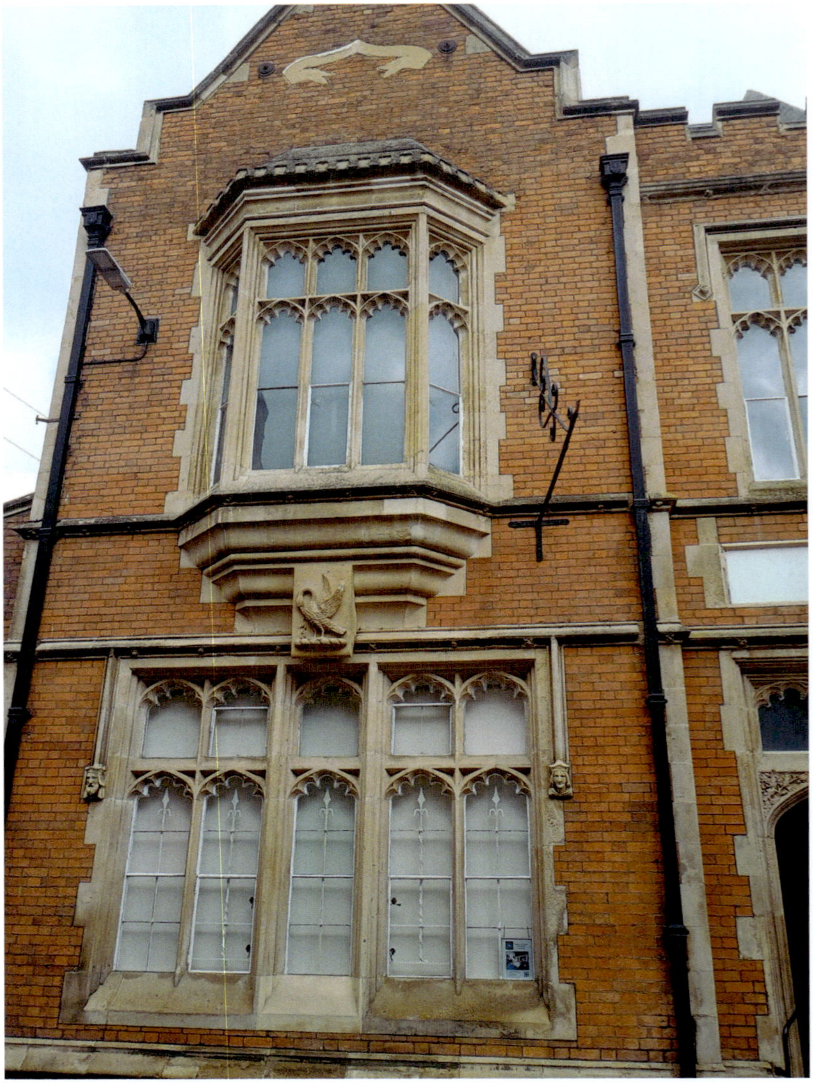

The former Lynn Savings Bank building. The Gothic design was meant to give a feeling of reassurance after some traumatic decades for banks.

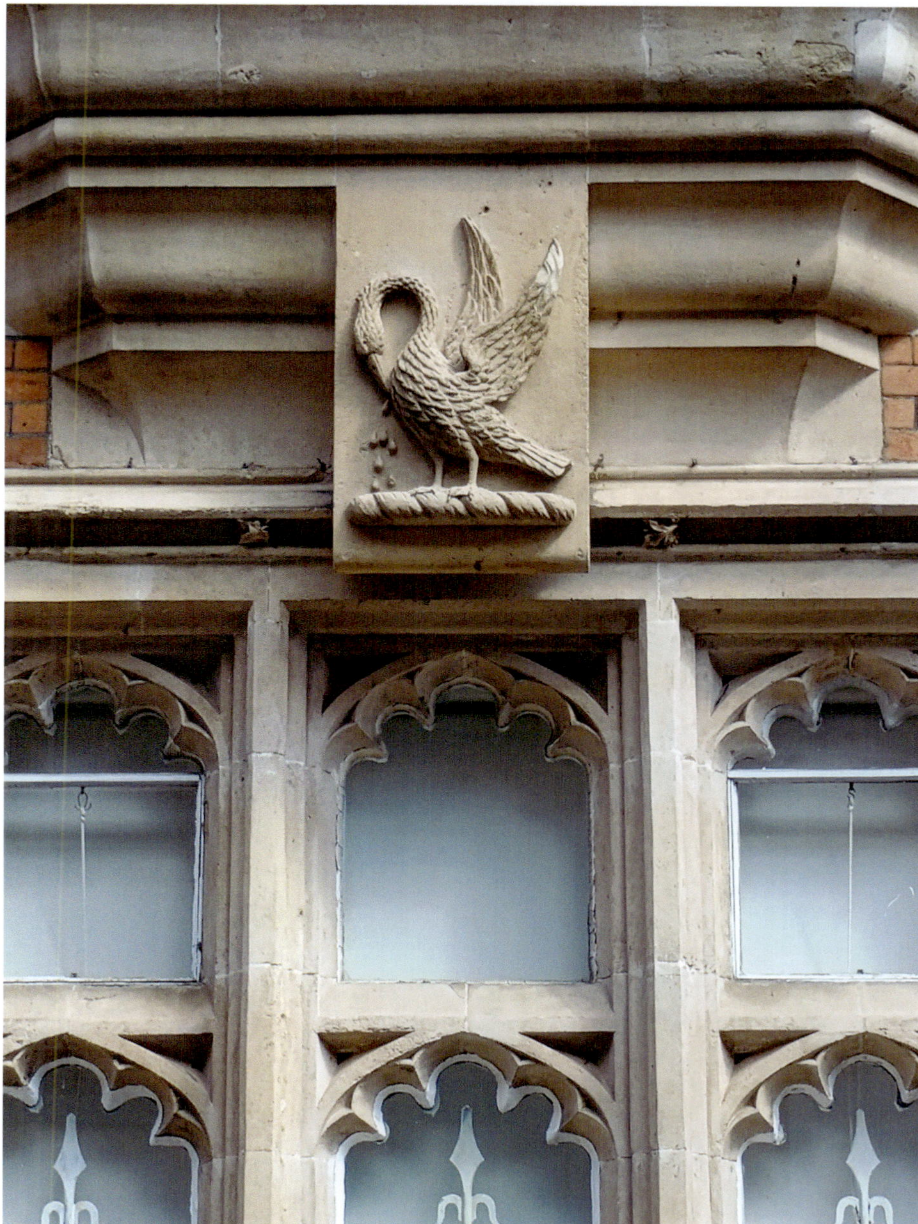

The pelican is a symbol associated with King's Lynn and can be found on the town's coat of arms.

Bank House

A stunning Grade II * listed Georgian townhouse, described by Sir Nikolaus Pevsner as one of the finest houses in King's Lynn, Bank House was built in the early eighteenth century for one of King's Lynn's richest merchants. Underneath the house extensive barrel-roofed vaults extend down to the river where wine imported from the continent would have been stored before being shipped on to Cambridge, Ely or the north. In the 1780s Joseph Gurney set up his first bank in Bank House. A dent is visible in the wooden floor of the Counting House, now the front room of the Brasserie, where nervous customers once shuffled their feet as they waited at the cashiers' desk to make their withdrawals. In 1809 the bank narrowly avoided being the first British bank to experience a 'run' by its investors. This was mainly as a consequence of the Bank of England's destabilising change of policy. As a result, one of the bank's partners had to ride in haste to Norwich to bring back gold to reassure the customers. In 1869 the bank moved to Tuesday Market Place. This building was then refronted in 1957 in the original style by the successor bank, Barclays. Fortunately, under the control of Samuel Gurney (1786–1856), banker and philanthropist, Gurney's recovered from this setback to become, via mergers and acquisitions, what is Barclays Bank today. Over the front door stands a fine statue of Charles I. The statue is said to have arrived in a wheelbarrow looking for a home when its original one in Tuesday Market Place was demolished.

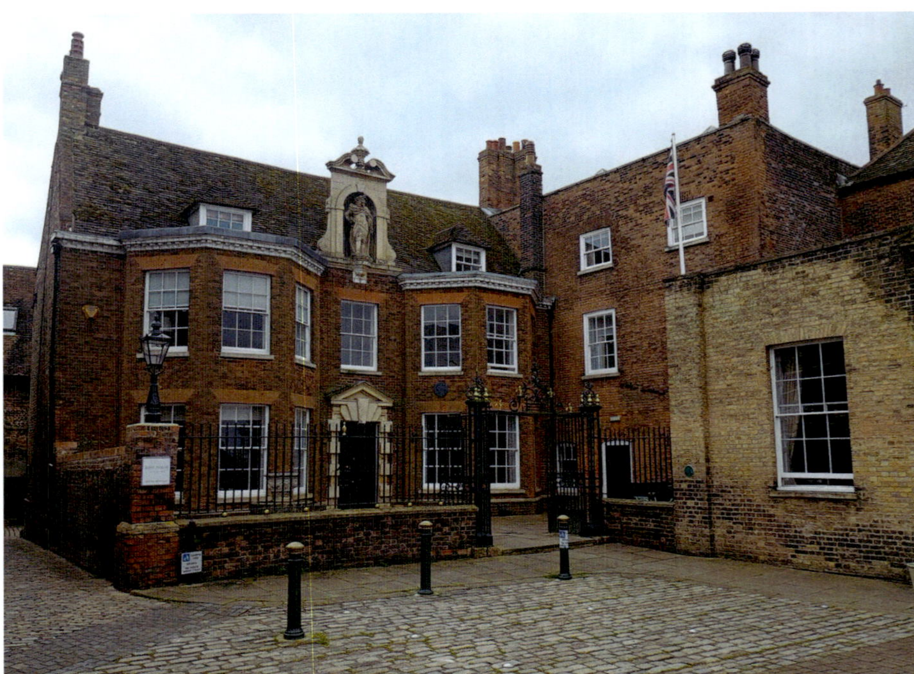

Bank House connects the £5 note, the North West Passage and Al Pacino.

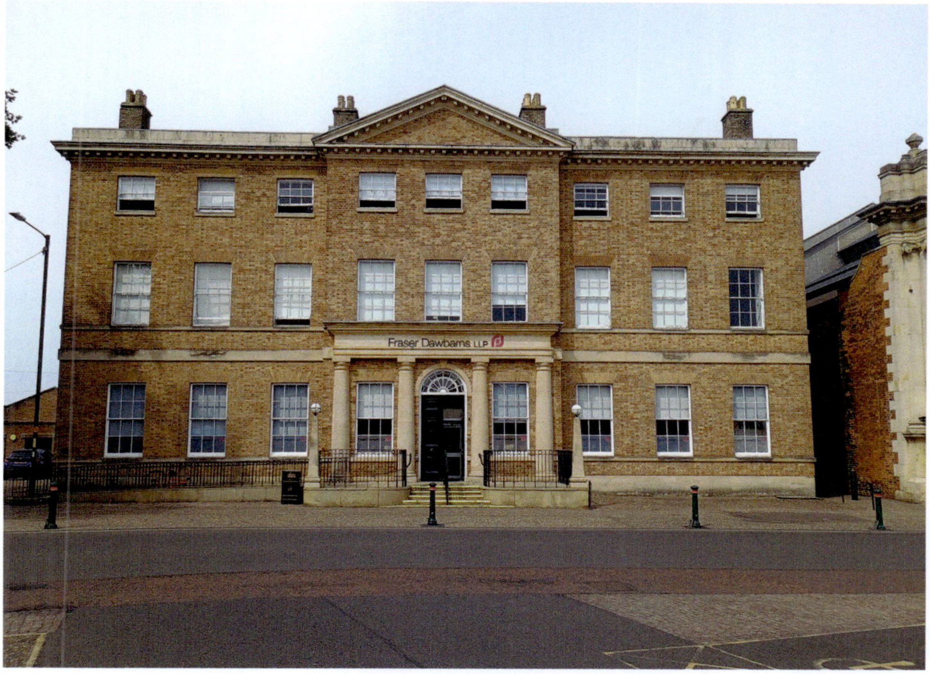

The magnificent former Gurney's Bank, providing a real sense of financial security.

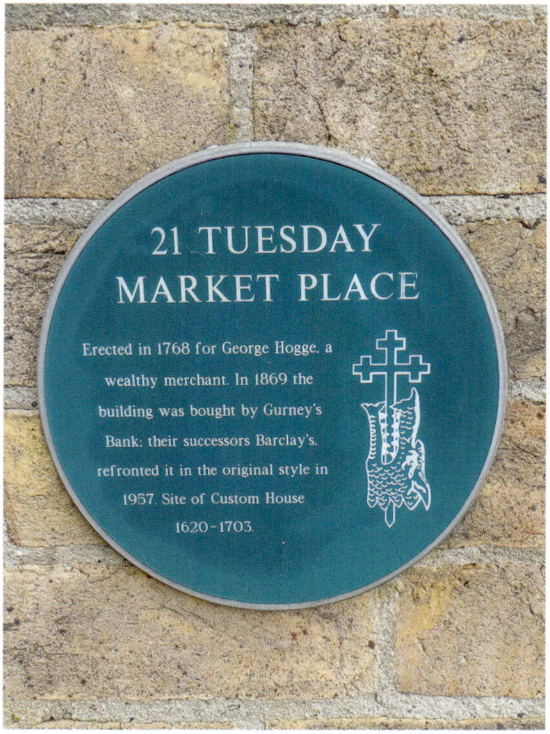

Plaque explaining the history of this glorious building.

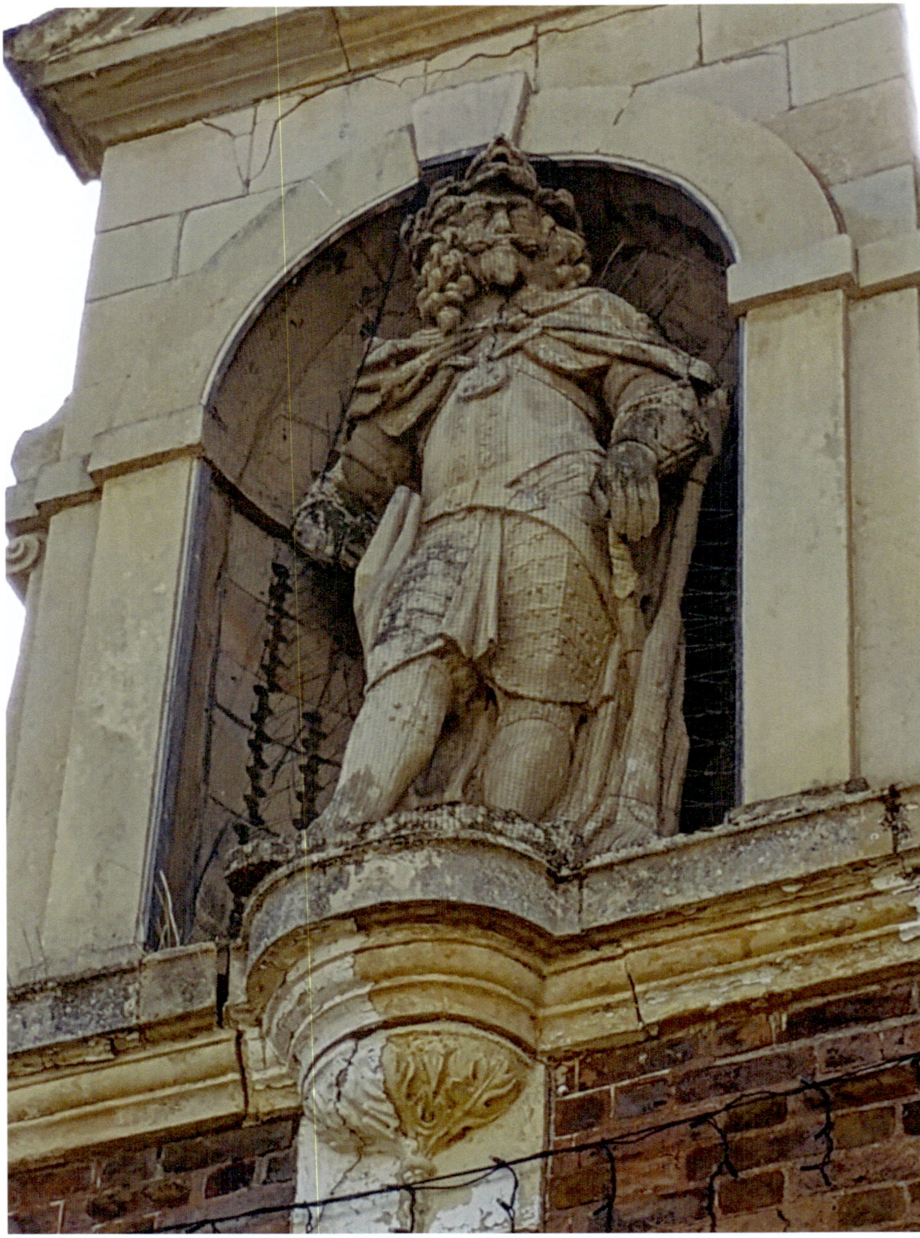

This king arrived in a wheelbarrow.

Captain Samuel Gurney Cresswell, the Arctic explorer and one of the first men to sail the North West Passage, was born in Bank House. After joining the navy as a boy, he ended up with Sir John McClure in 1849 on a trip to find both the North West Passage and Sir John Franklin's ship that had not returned from its own search to find the elusive route through the northern ice. Cresswell was appointed as the second lieutenant and ship's artist aboard HMS *Investigator* for the expedition. The *Investigator* ended up being trapped in ice for two years and eventually it was decided to abandon ship in 1853. Cresswell, along with twenty-four invalids, followed his commander, McClure, on a 170-mile trek to Kellett's winter camp located off Melville Island. Because he was in good health, Cresswell volunteered to continue overland for about another 300 miles to Beechey Island in the hope of meeting a ship. In the process he discovered and crossed the route that had eluded other sailors. Luckily, he succeeded in making the epic sledging journey and also actually managed to find a ship home. Cresswell set sail for home in August 1853 with proof of the existence of the North West Passage and the acclaim of being one of the first naval officers to cross it. On 26 October 1853, a public dinner was held in Cresswell's honour at the King's Lynn Assembly Rooms, organised by his native townsmen. Tickets were one guinea each. In gratitude for his safe delivery home, he gave money for the creation of a new east window in St Margaret's Church. He died on 14 August 1867 and is buried in All Saints' churchyard, North Runcton. Elizabeth Fry (née Gurney), the prison reformer, whose formidable profile appears on the back of the £5 note, was his grandmother and stayed in the house on many occasions when visiting her daughter. In later years the house became offices for tax inspectors, lawyers and shipbrokers. In 1985 it was used as the centrepiece of the epic flop *Revolution,* starring Al Pacino and Donald Sutherland. After a time as a beautiful private home, offering bed & breakfast, Bank House came on the market in 2007 and was transformed into the current business. After nearly fifteen years in September 2023, it was put up for sale again.

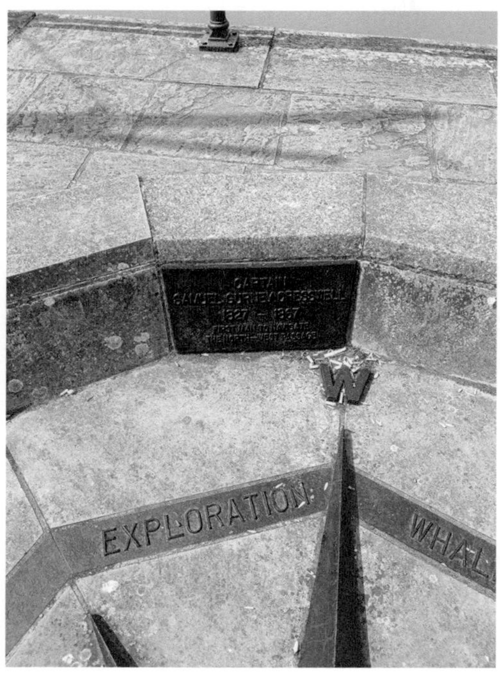

On the Purfleet Quay there is a compass rose with plaques commemorating eight significant people with links to King's Lynn. This one honours Samuel Gurney Cresswell.

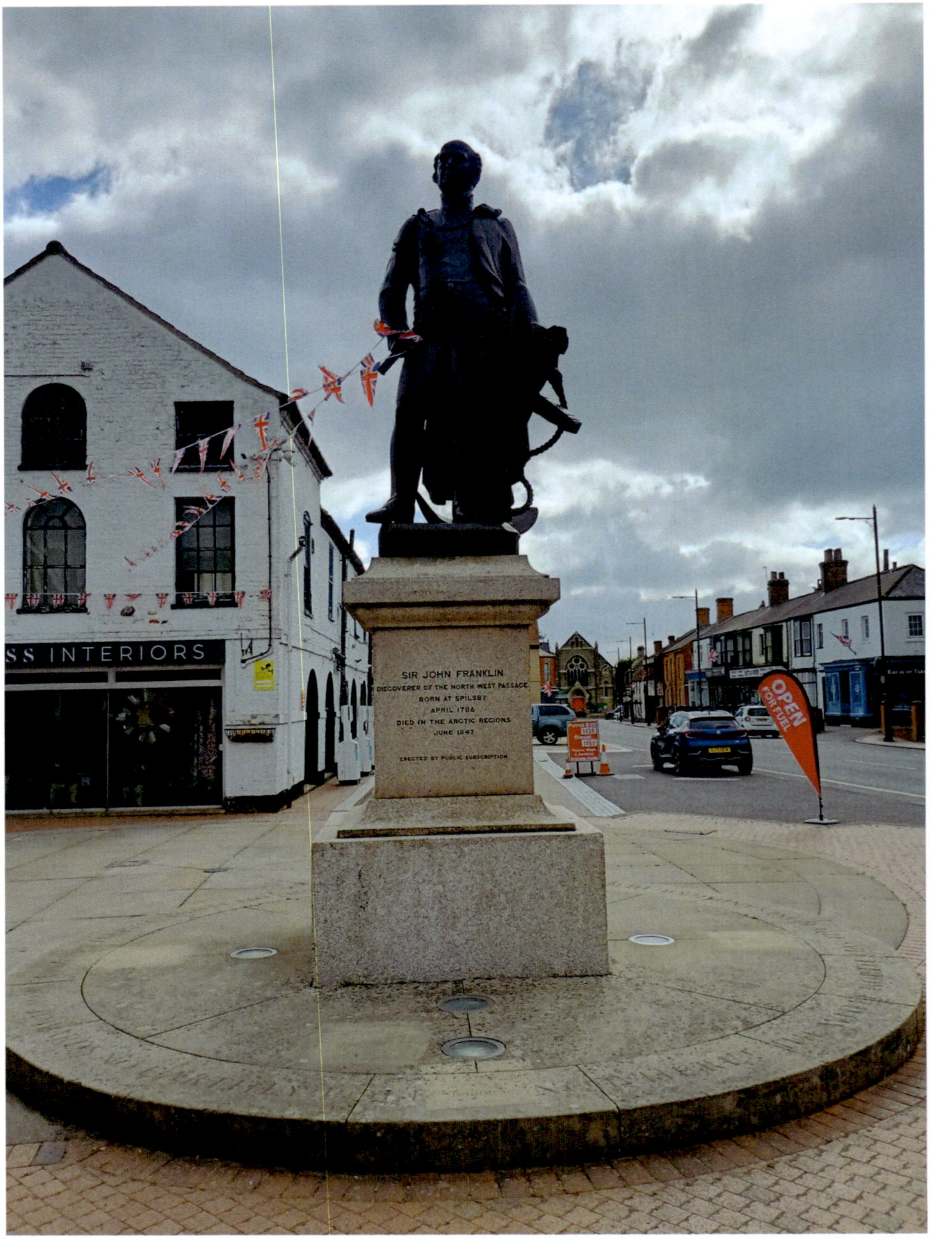

Sir John Franklin (1786–1847) statue in Spilsby, Lincolnshire. After his last ill-fated expedition, reports from local Inuit and later archaeological and osteological research suggest that some of the last survivors resorted to consuming human remains as a desperate measure in the face of starvation.

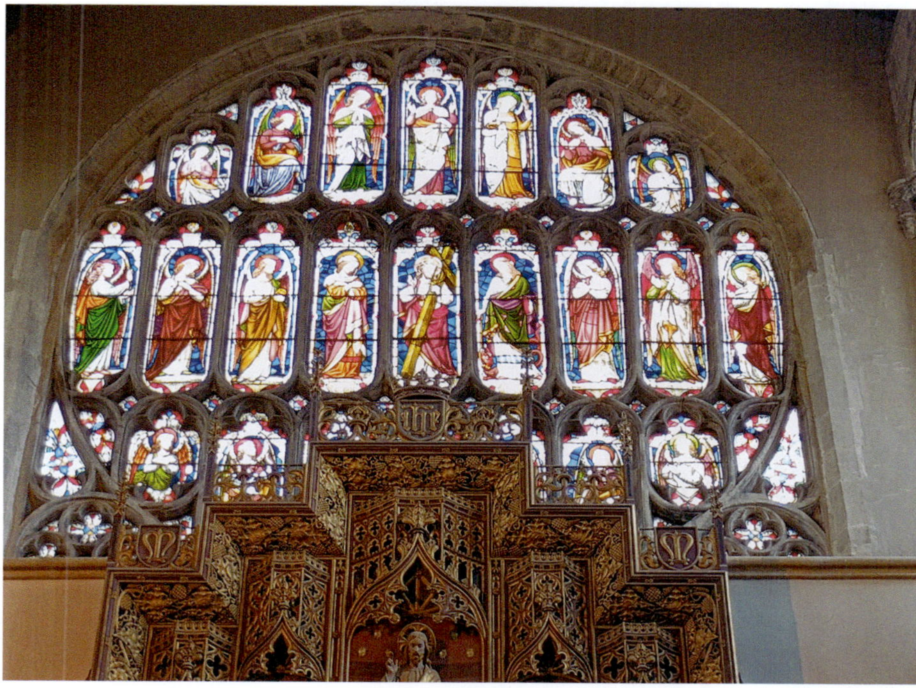

In gratitude for his safe delivery home, Cresswell gave money for the creation of a magnificent new east window in St Margaret's Church.

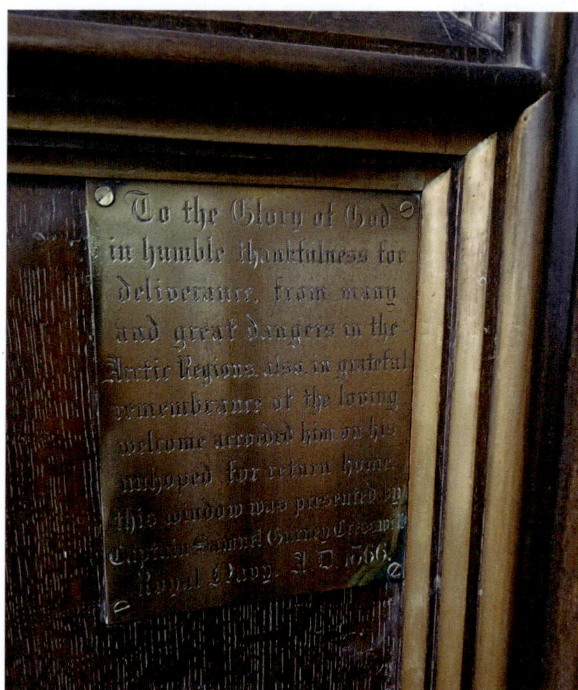

Dedication plaque below the east window. The window was presented by Cresswell in 1866, a year before he passed away in the historic town.

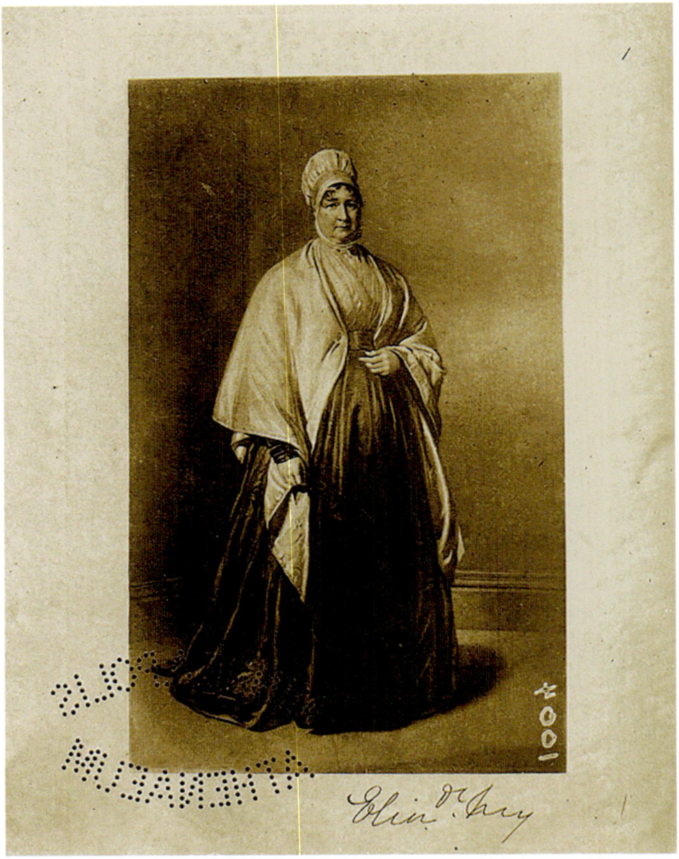

Elizabeth Fry (1780–1845), Quaker preacher and philanthropist. She was depicted on the British £5 note between 2002 and 2017. American National Red Cross photograph collection *c.* 1918. (Library of Congress)

Thoresby College

Thoresby College was built just after 1500 by Thomas Thoresby, wealthy merchant and former mayor. Originally called Trinity College, it housed a community of priests appointed by the town's Trinity Guild. Thomas Thoresby set up what was known as a chantry, an organisation to pay people to regularly, and in perpetuity, pray for certain other people when they were alive and when they were dead. Thoresby College was established, the 'college' just being accommodation for the priests who would be required to do the praying. Thoresby funded the building and the salaries and set up land to provide an income so that the praying could go on long after his death. Thoresby believed in both the reality of suffering in purgatory after passing away and the effectiveness of prayer by others on your behalf in relieving and shortening that time of suffering. He did this because he believed there was a direct link between the number of prayers that were said for him and the amount of time he would spend in purgatory. It was a system to help reduce his jeopardy and help him get out of spiritual gaol. The system was both impressive and tragic. Before his death he employed sixteen priests; thirteen were to pray for members of the

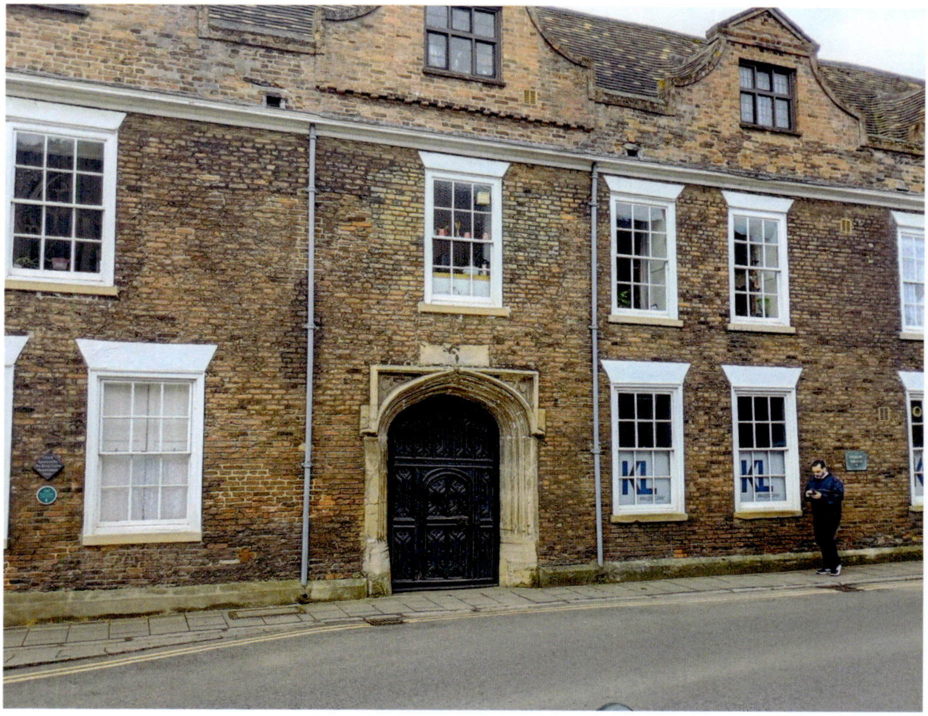

Thoresby College from Queen Street. This is where perpetuity lasted less than forty years.

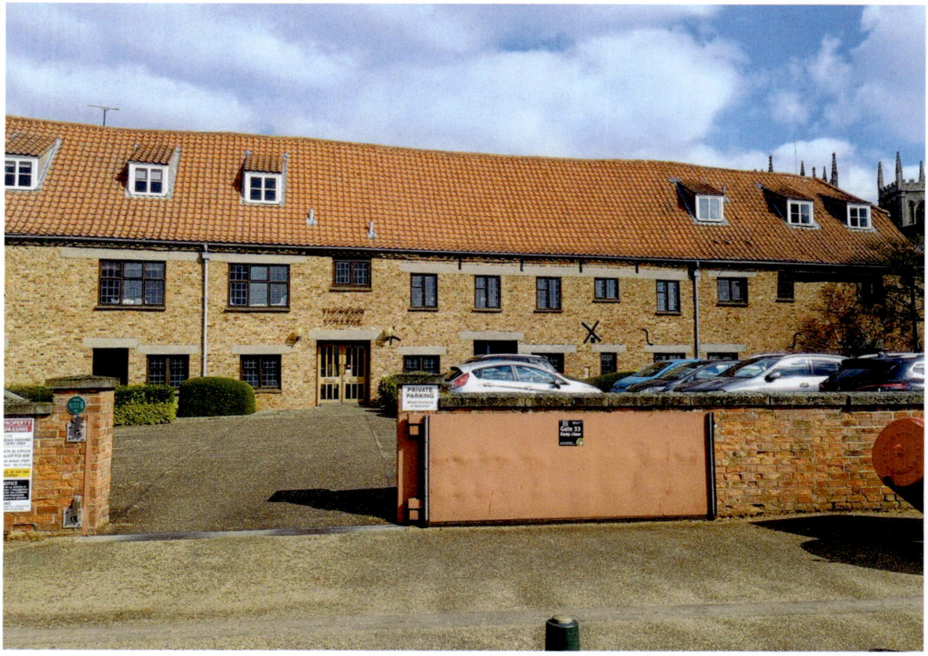

Thoresby College from South Quay. A college was accommodation for priests.

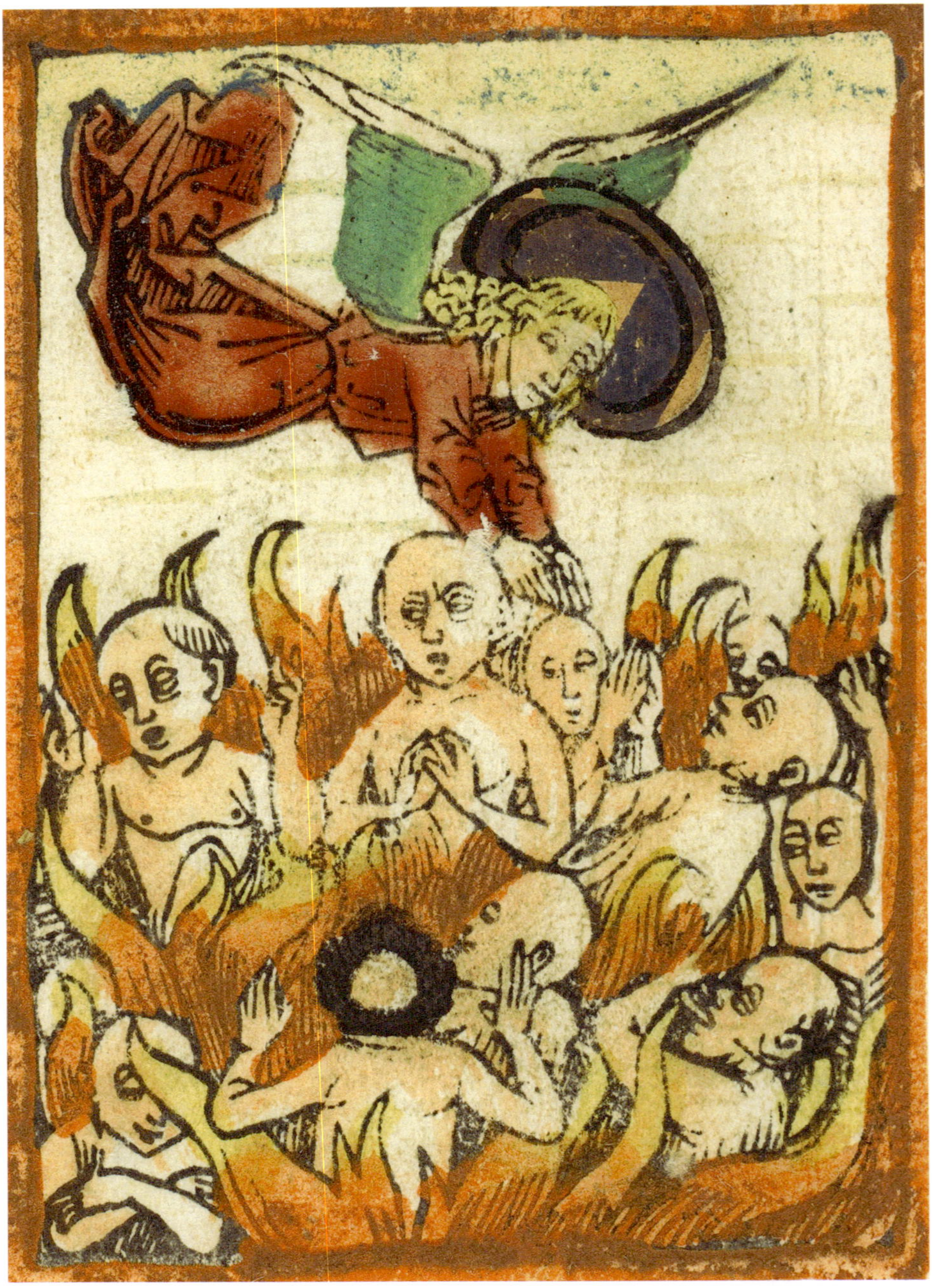

'Purgatory', fifteenth-century German woodcut. Purgatory is the place where the soul is cleansed of all impurities, as Dante described in his poem *The Divine Comedy*. (National Gallery of Art)

Holy Trinity Guild, of which he was a member, two were to pray for him and his immediate family, and one priest was to teach six boys Latin. Thoresby was not a selfish man. It is important to realise that in his time, Thoresby was also not an unusual man. Many rich men were leaving endowments to ensure that they were regularly prayed for after death. It was quite usual for monarchs to spend fortunes to ensure that large numbers were paid to pray for their souls after death. For example, Henry V left enough money for 20,000 masses to be said within a year for his soul, and Richard III funded a chantry chapel in York Minster to be staffed by hundreds of praying clergy. The tragedy is that although the chantry was completed around the time of Thoresby's death in 1510, in 1547 it was closed by Edward VI, who also closed another 2,373. The grand oak door had Thoresby's name carved into it. Above that door was a Latin inscription that translated to 'Pray for the soul of Thomas Thoresby'. When the Reformation came about the first three words were hacked away. His 'perpetuity' was relatively short. From 1547 onwards, whoever was praying for the souls of the dead, it was not members of the relatively new Church of England. It would not be people in Thoresby's now defunct chantry.

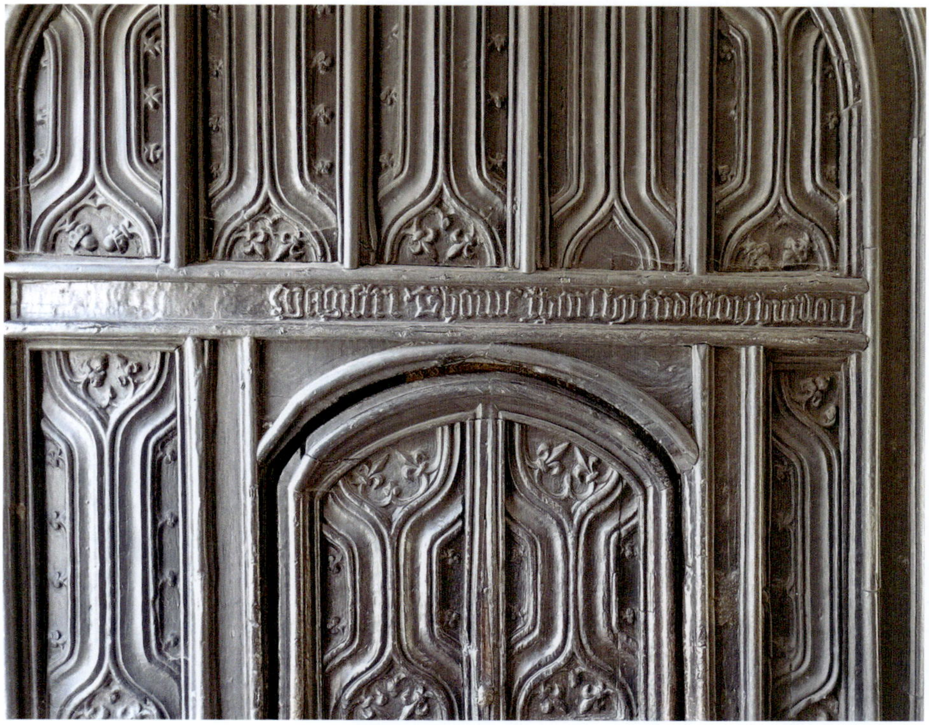

This grand oak door had a Latin inscription that translated to 'Pray for the soul of Thomas Thoresby'. When the Reformation came about the first three words were hacked away.

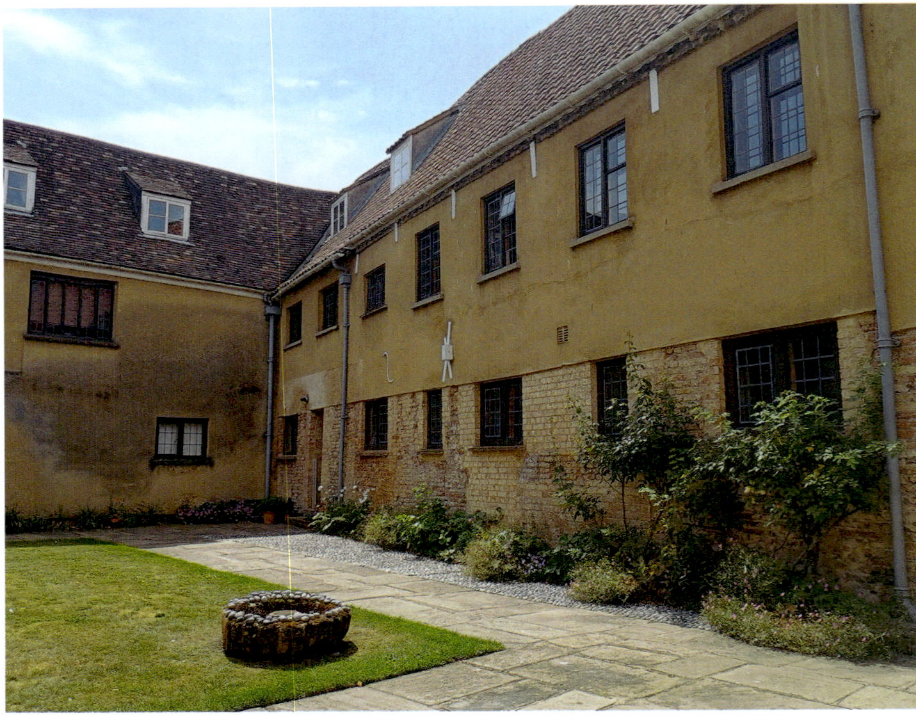

The tranquil and peaceful courtyard of Thoresby College.

In 1547, therefore, after the Reformation the college was sold and subsequently underwent adaption for domestic and commercial use. As a result, the original internal arrangements of the college have been obscured. Nevertheless, ranged around its open quadrangle, Thoresby College is one of the most complete survivals of medieval Lynn. Despite many uses over the ensuing centuries, the footprint of the medieval building remains unchanged with many original features surviving, including the fine roof of the Great Hall. In 1963 the entire complex was bought by Ruth, Lady Fermoy, and her daughter, Viscountess Althorpe (later Mrs Shand-Kydd) and presented to the King's Lynn Preservation Trust for restoration, with the request that the building be used for the benefit of the whole community. The building was saved and restored by the trust between 1963 and 1968. Today the north, east and south ranges of the college are divided into domestic flats and offices. The central courtyard features a Judas Tree (*Cersis siliquastrum*), so named because it is reputed to be the tree from which Judas Iscariot hanged himself. The Great Hall and Lower Hall in the west range are available for hire and they are popular venues for local organisations. Thoresby College is also home to the King's Lynn Preservation Trust office.

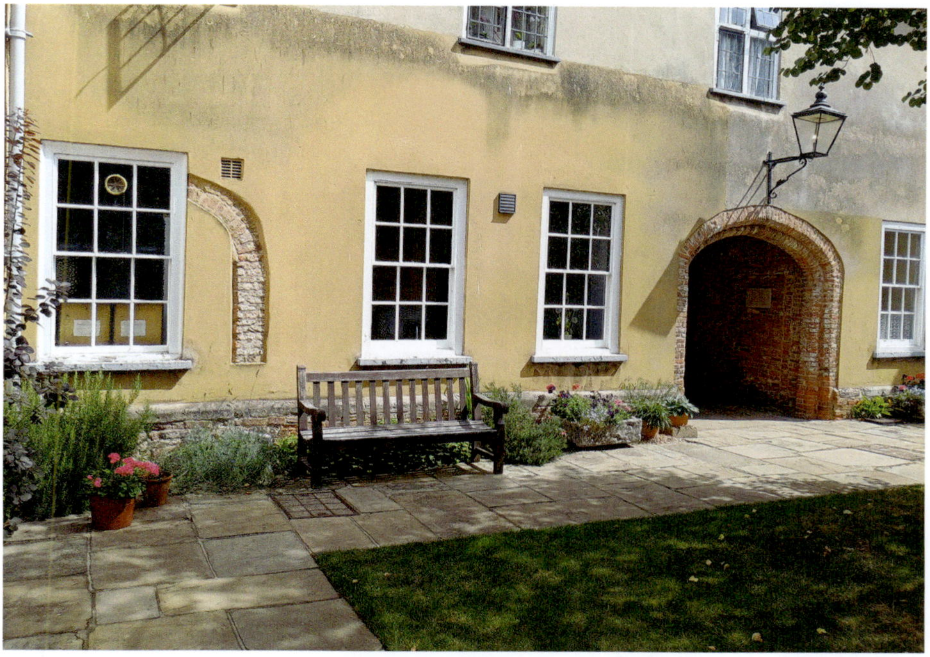

Above: A calm area of seclusion amidst the bustle of the medieval quarter.

Right: The central courtyard features a Judas Tree (*Cersis siliquastrum*).

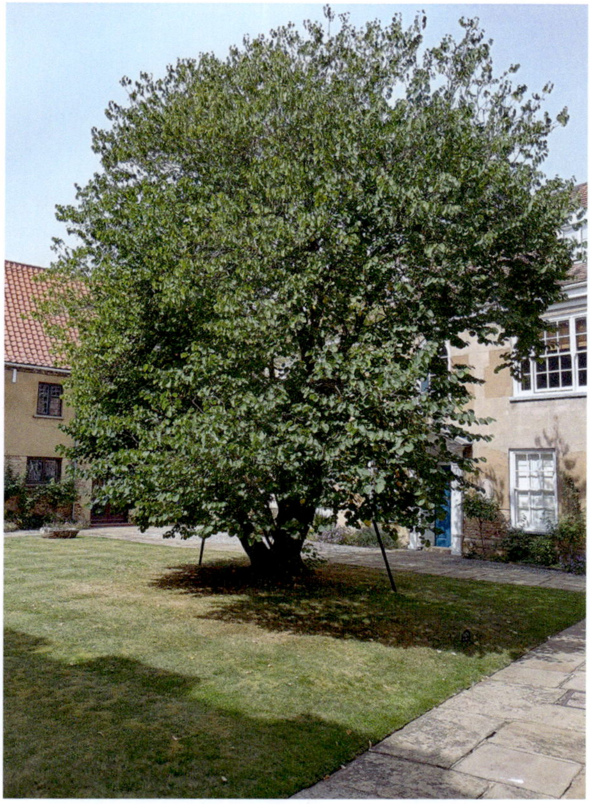

Red Mount Chapel

During the medieval period, the Shrine of Our Lady of Walsingham was the second most popular goal for pilgrimages in England after Canterbury. It was also one of the most common destinations for pilgrims from across Europe. They flocked to visit the small Norfolk village of Little Walsingham, and their route from the European continent took them through the port of King's Lynn. The striking Red Mount Chapel is one of the most peculiar late medieval Gothic

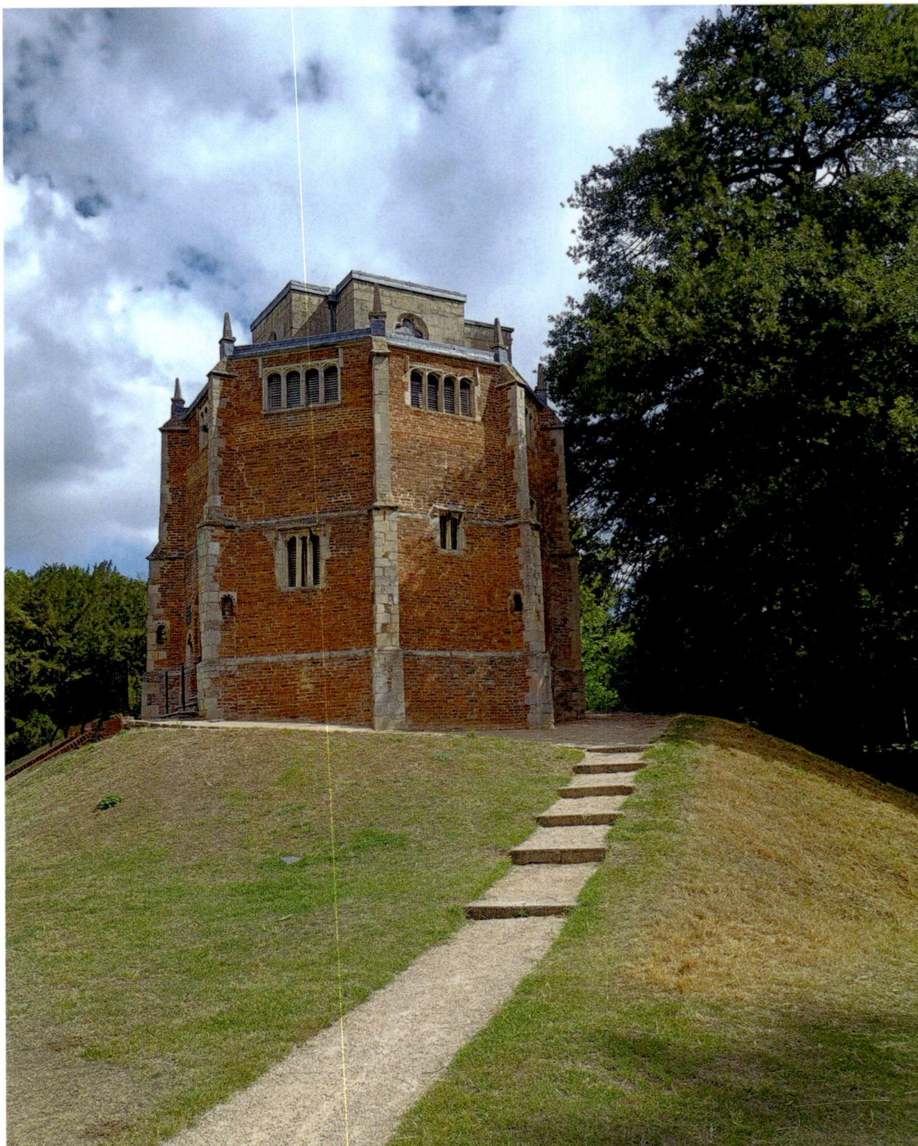

Red Mount Chapel. A unique one-way system in a multiuse building.

structures in England. It is built to an octagonal plan and stands three storeys high. It is supported by buttresses rising two storeys, and each buttress is pierced by a hole that forms a statue niche. It is made of two concentric drums rising over a barrel-vaulted cellar. Brick staircases run inside the wall formed by the two drums. The two staircases run counter-wise to each other, arriving at the chapel antechamber from opposite directions This is because it was so popular that the steps were designed so the pilgrims did not have to cross each other going up and down. It is a unique one-way system. The bottom two storeys are made of red brick, but the top storey is built from stone. It was probably added several decades after the base. There is a priest's room and two chapels, a lower chapel and an upper chapel. The upper chapel is decorated with a stunning fan-vaulted ceiling in ornate late Perpendicular Gothic style. This ceiling has been likened to the world's largest fan-vaulted stone ceiling in the King's College Chapel, Cambridge, which is not surprising if the same master mason was involved in both.

Red Mount Chapel has been part of King's Lynn's history for an impressive 540 years. In that time, it has survived the Reformation, the Civil War, and two world wars and it still stands strong today. In 1483 a plan was proposed by Robert Curraunt to build a respite for pilgrims on their way to the Shrine of Our Lady at Walsingham giving them the chance to stop and pray. Two years later, his request was granted, with an official document stating: 'It is agreed by alle that Robert Curraunt shall have licence to bilde a chapel upon the mount called the Ladye Hylle'. The Benedictine prior of King's Lynn was granted a lease of land to build on and Curraunt soon put his plan into action. It was agreed that the Red Mount earthwork, which had been constructed as part of the medieval town's defences, would make a perfect spot for the new chapel. Originally named 'the Chapel of St Mary on the Mount', it only carried out its role as a place of worship for fifty years. In 1536, when Henry VIII passed the Suppression of Religious Houses Act, all monasteries with an income of less than £200 were forced to close. Luckily, Red Mount Chapel was only partially dismantled, unlike many other monasteries; in fact, by 1540 almost forty monasteries a month were being torn down. Parts of the roof and brickwork were taken by labourers for other buildings, and by 1573 it had been thoroughly defaced and left roofless, a shell of its former self.

However, it was not to remain lifeless for long. In 1642 the broken building was given an entirely different purpose, marking the beginning of a turbulent new chapter in its story. The English Civil War had just begun, and the Royalists in King's Lynn were trapped, blockaded by the River Ouse and surrounded on land by Parliamentarians. The town was still a vital trading port, considered too strategically important to be overlooked, and was eventually captured by Cromwell's forces. The Parliamentarians soon began improving King's Lynn's medieval defences and building new fortifications, transforming it into one of the strongest fortresses in East Anglia. Red Mount Chapel played a crucial role within the town over the course of the war. Its high vantage point made it a brilliant location for lookouts, and soldiers stashed up to eighteen barrels of volatile gunpowder within its walls. On quiet days where no fighting commenced, the soldiers carved their initials into the brickwork whilst others drew buildings with little flags on top. The oldest piece of graffiti dates back to 1639, pre-dating the Civil War. The soldiers seemingly noticed it and took it upon themselves to do the same, leaving their own less violent mark on King's Lynn.

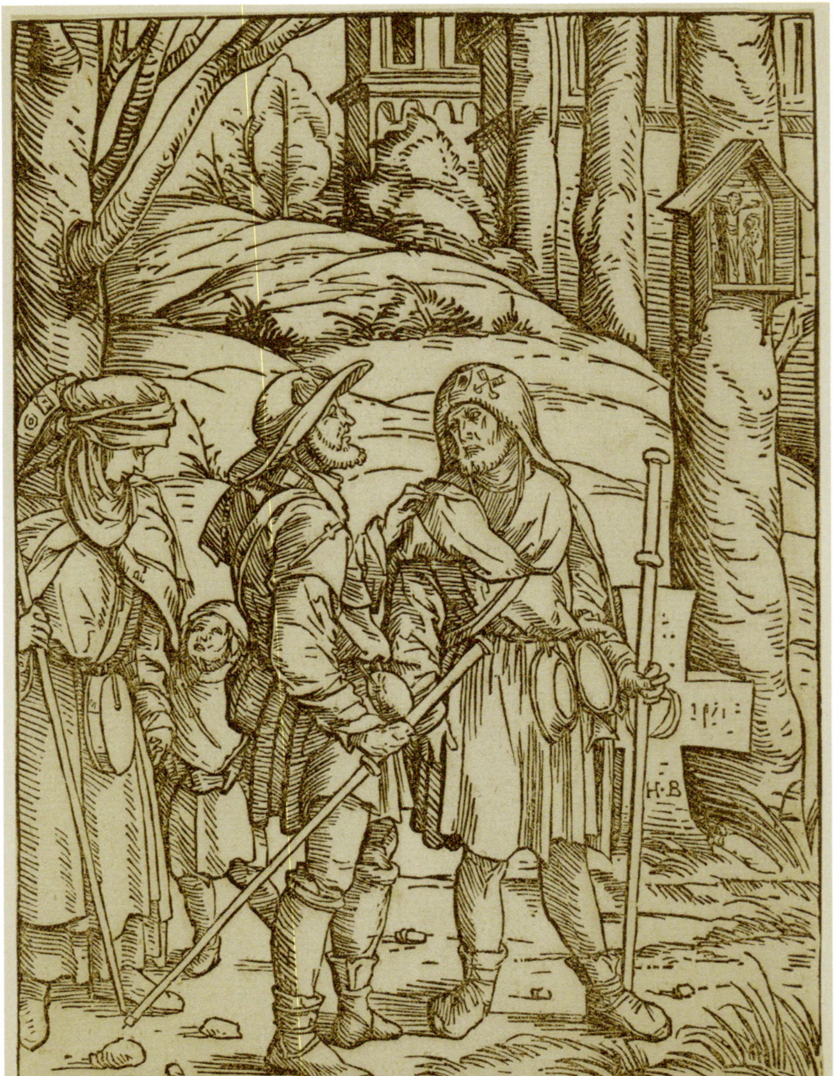

Pilgrims at a Wayside Shrine, 1508, by German artist Hans Burgkmair (1473–1531). (National Gallery of Art)

The chapel's next occupation after the Civil War was a considerably grim one. In 1665 the worst outbreak of plague struck England since the Black Death in 1348, later gaining the description 'The Great Plague'. It killed roughly 15 per cent of London's population, reaching its peak in September when 7,165 Londoners died in a week. The whole country was plagued, including King's Lynn. Red Mount Chapel was repurposed as a charnel house, a place for the dead to be stored far away from the living. Thankfully, the outbreak of 1665 was the last instance of plague in the United Kingdom, enabling the chapel to be used for less unsettling purposes. A century later, the chapel's prominent position and missing roof attracted the attention of students keen to study the stars. Parts of the building were repaired so it could be used as an observatory for teaching navigation, making way for some truly awe-inspiring evenings. By the 1800s the chapel was in a poor state, but fortunately funds were raised to restore the building to its former glory. The outer windows were replaced, the floors and stairs were repaired and there was even a stained-glass window installed in the upper floor, taken from St Nicholas' Chapel in King's Lynn. It was once again a magnificent landmark in The Walks, so eye-catching that the artist Thomas Baines dedicated a painting to it. Simply titled *Red Mount Chapel*, it is an atmospheric view of the monument from the river, providing clear proof that it was as striking back then as it is today.

The building has been the very definition of resilience throughout the past 540 years, even surviving the half-ton German bomb that struck The Walks in 1942. Given its historical significance, it is no surprise that Red Mount Chapel was given funding by the National Lottery Heritage Fund in 2007 to be fully restored and repaired. A year later it became one of the 2.5 per cent of Listed Buildings in the country to be given Grade I status, securing its survival long into the future, hopefully for another five centuries. Separate tunnels are said to run to and from the chapel to Greyfriars Tower and the 'White Hart', in St James Street. This pub was refurbished and then reopened under new ownership in November 2023. The hostelry can be found in an historic part of the town and is the oldest continuously licenced public house in King's Lynn. There is still some thirteenth- and fourteenth-century brickwork on show. It is said to be haunted by a ghostly monk, possibly from the nearby St Margaret's Church. The phantom is described as a shadowy, hooded figure. The church and pub were once connected by yet another now bricked-up tunnel.

A tale surrounding the Red Mount Chapel describes how a man went exploring rumoured passageways in the vicinity of the building. He played his fiddle so that observers above ground could follow his progress. Soon, the music stopped and the man was never seen again, but his companion, a dog, returned to the surface to greet the man's friends. Sadly, this is a story that is repeated across the length of the United Kingdom with some variations. One particularly regional tale features a piper walking in a cave towards the Devils

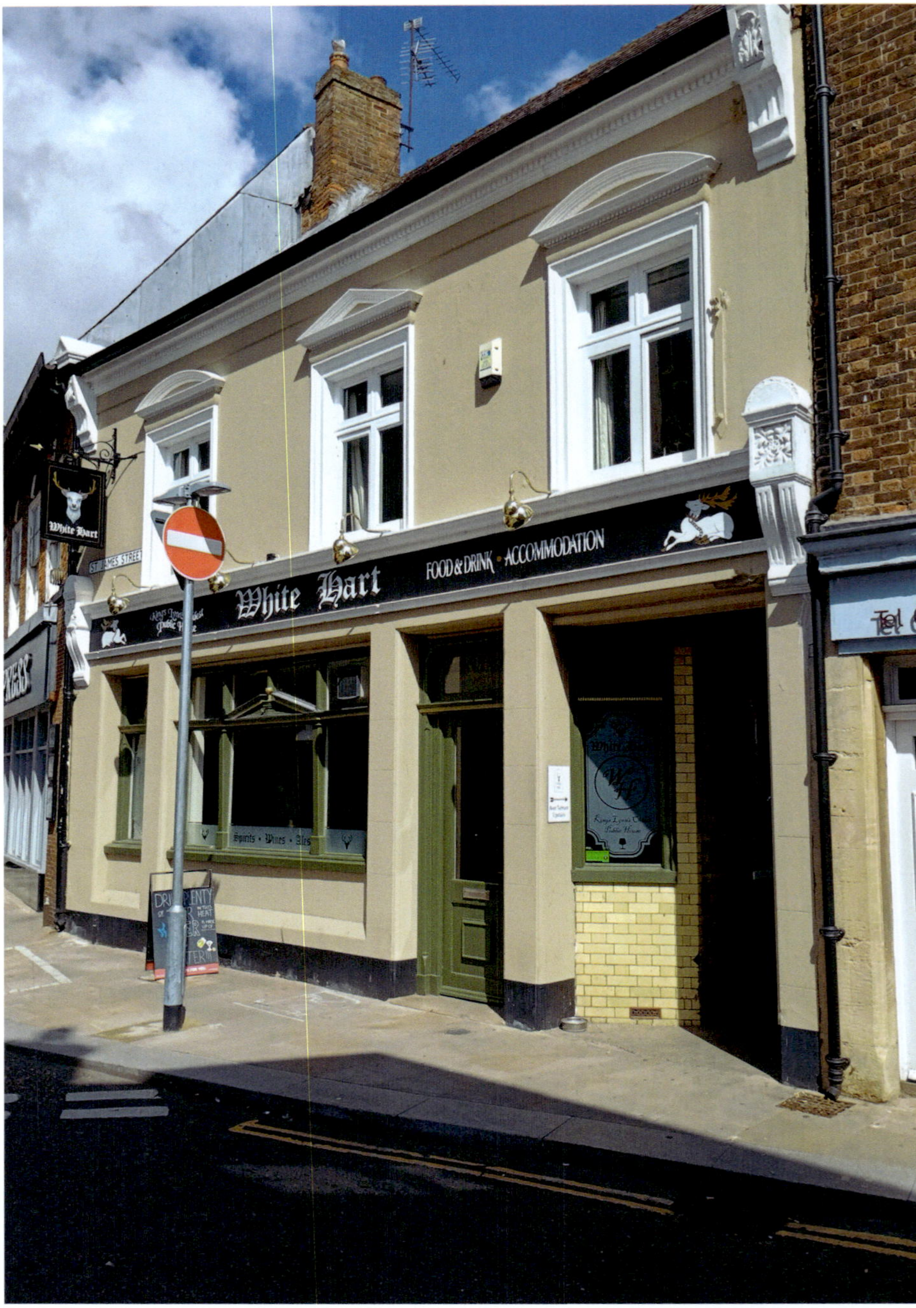

White Hart on St James Street, one of the many 'stops' on the King's Lynn underground?

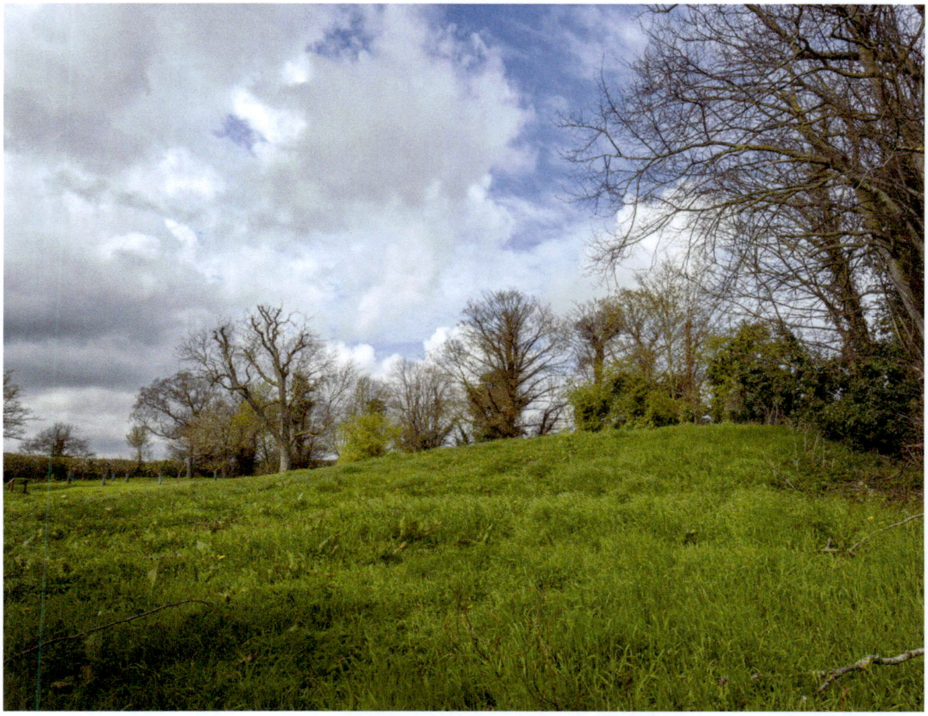

Fiddlers Hill. An ancient barrow full of secrets? (Courtesy of Norfolk Archaeological Trust https://www.norfarchtrust.org.uk/)

Cauldron in Galloway then disappearing. This features in S. R. Crockett's 1911 novel *The Smugglers*. A more local and intriguing version occurred less than 20 miles away from the Red Mount Chapel at Fiddlers Hill, Wareham, Norfolk. This famous legend tells of a mysterious tunnel that supposedly ran through the centre of the hill, reaching from Blakeney Guildhall to Binham Priory. The hill is a prehistoric burial mound, or 'barrow'. The supposed tunnel quickly became a source of fear, as well as secrets. There were rumours of a yet another spectral, black-robed monk that stalked the priory grounds. Nobody was willing to venture into the tunnel to solve the mystery. Then a fiddler stepped up to the plate. He would go down into the tunnels while playing his instrument, so that the townsfolk could follow him above ground. But when they got to the hill, his music abruptly stopped. There were all sorts of rumours. Some said that the Devil had taken him. The site was given its current name to commemorate his sudden disappearance. Sightings of the black-robed monk continue to this day, while the centre of Fiddlers Hill has never been excavated. However, in April 1933, a host of national and regional newspapers reported that Norfolk County Council roadmen, carrying out junction improvements at the Fiddlers Hill crossroads, had discovered the skeletons of a man and his dog. The bones were handed over to the police who took them to Doctor Hicks at Wells-next-the-Sea for examination. They were to be seen later by an anthropologist. Although this story was repeated again in exactly the same wording by some newspapers in 1937 on an obviously slow news day, intriguingly no update appears to have been made since.

On a more real-world footing, the Red Mount Chapel was opened on 8 September 2024 as a part of Heritage Open Days and it is to be hoped that this access will be repeated in subsequent years.

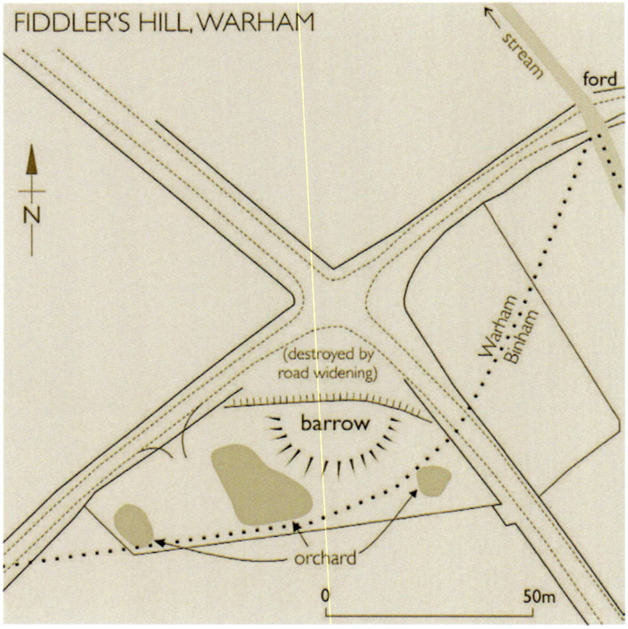

Plan of the road widening which unearthed a greater mystery. (Courtesy of Norfolk Archaeological Trust https://www.norfarchtrust.org.uk/)